WEST-
FEVER

WEST-FEVER

Brian W. Dippie

Introduction by James H. Nottage

Autry Museum of Western Heritage • Los Angeles, California

in association with

University of Washington Press • Seattle, Washington and London, United Kingdom

Library of Congress Cataloging-in-Publication Data

Dippie, Brian W.
     West-fever / Brian W. Dippie ; introduction by James H. Nottage.
         p.   cm.
     Includes bibliographical references (p.   ).
     ISBN 0-295-97735-3 (hardcover). — ISBN 1-882880-07-2 (softcover). —
ISBN 1-882880-08-0 (limited)
     1. West (U.S.)—Social life and customs—Catalogs. 2. Frontier
and pioneer life—West (U.S.)—Catalogs. 3. West (U.S.) in art—
Catalogs. 4. Cowboys—West (U.S.)—History—Catalogs. 5. Material
culture—West (U.S.)—Catalogs. 6. Popular culture—West (U.S.)—
Catalogs. 7. Autry Museum of Western Heritage—Catalogs.
I. Autry Museum of Western Heritage. II. Title.
     F591.D57 1998
978—dc21

                                                            98-13528
                                                            CIP

ISBN: 0-295-97735-3 (hardcover)
          1-882880-07-2 (softcover)
          1-882880-08-0 (limited edition)

Project managed by: Suzanne G. Fox

Designed by: Matt Hahn, ThinkDesign

Photography by: Susan Einstein, Los Angeles, California, unless otherwise noted.

Printed and bound in Hong Kong through Empowering Partners Incorporated, USA

INSIDE FRONT COVER (DETAIL)
Thomas Moran (1837-1926)
Mountain of the Holy Cross, 1875
Oil on canvas
Donated by Mr. and Mrs. Gene Autry

Is it really the West? Don Teodoro de Croix served as Governor General of the interior provinces of New Spain from 1776 to 1783. For many moving north from Mexico the region did not have the Western identity that Americans applied to it years later. M. L. Ynchaustequi (active in Lima, Peru, 1790s). *Don Teodoro de Croix*, ca. 1790.

FOREWORD

ILLUMINATING THE TERRAIN

When the Autry Museum of Western Heritage opened to the public in November 1988, its creators had been focused for several years on the institutional mission to explore the broad temporal, topical and geographical elements of the history and peoples of the West. At the same time, they were not surprised that some members of the public would expect the museum to be a monument to the life and personal memorabilia of recording, broadcasting, film and performing legend Gene Autry.

As a philanthropist the Singing Cowboy had long wanted to create a museum as a gesture, a way to leave something behind. Perhaps the result of his dream goes beyond what he originally imagined. Certainly within the boundaries of the museum galleries the West presented is broader and more comprehensive than original plans called for. In 1985 and 1986 there was room to dream in creating the museum. Just as with a book, the exhibits were conceived as ways to tell a story. Objects and art works would be the central features describing the region we think of as the West, from prehistoric roots to the present. The impact of art, performance and advertising in manipulating perceptions of the West would be contrasted with those elements of real experience. There was not a pre-existing collection, so research and design proceeded to fill more than 50,000 square feet of exhibit space, at least on paper, with ideal artifacts imagined to tell the story. The challenge, then, was to go out and find art and artifacts to fulfill their specific roles.

Hard work, good fortune, strategic loans and supportive donors made success, for the most part, possible. When the museum opened to the public after three years of planning the cases and walls were filled according to blueprints with ideal objects. Therefore, the exhibited collection was given a context by the story told in the galleries. This was, of course, just one interpretation. In the years since, the collection has grown, changes have been made in the galleries and new visions of the staff and academic and community advisors have broadened and sharpened the scope of the institution's holdings.

Perspective and context for any museum collection can come from different sources. Academic discipline, gender, occupation, racial and cultural perspective, religious and political focus and individual intellect all allow us to perceive and understand different meanings, contexts and values for the art and artifacts collected and preserved by the museum. *West-Fever* presents the thoughts of an admired colleague on a portion of a collection that now numbers more than 40,000 objects. As the Autry Museum of Western Heritage continues to grow, as we assess our first ten years, others will be asked to examine the collection and to provide additional "contexts for the collection." Continued study, self evaluation and advisors help to reveal areas where the collection is weak, where interpretations are lax, where growth needs to occur.

There are countless realities in the Western story that go well beyond the sources of myth. Those real things that Professor Dippie describes herein as the "enemies of myth" are found in the objects of diverse communities; these give substance to fact and experience. Dippie has delivered readers to the heart of the Autry Museum's larger purpose when he writes that "an inclusive West will have to make room for the Old as well as the New, the mythic as well as the mundane—for comedy as well as tragedy." The everyday artifacts of differing experiences and perspectives are indeed the basis for understanding the realities of the Western experience for everyone.

One valid question is, "Whose West is it?" Perhaps therein lies not just the rest of the story, but the motivation for the second ten years of the Autry Museum. Planning for this volume drew toward completion as Gene Autry celebrated his 90th birthday. Our founding President and Chief Executive Officer, Joanne Hale, is driving toward conceptualizing the institution's second ten years. Hand in hand with Jackie Autry, she has made it possible for goals to be met and exceeded. They, along with the board of directors, the national advisory council, the staff, volunteers and docents, present here the stimulating thoughts of Brian Dippie, who serves up what lies at the heart of any museum— the collection. It is a course that is at once satisfying. If you hunger for more, it will be served in due time.

JAMES H. NOTTAGE
VICE PRESIDENT AND CHIEF CURATOR

ABOVE

Whose West is it? This Hmong story quilt, from the 1980s, tells how one family moved from Laos, Cambodia, to California. It is an overland document in the same sense as the diary of a gold rush pioneer who traveled over the Oregon Trail to California in 1849.

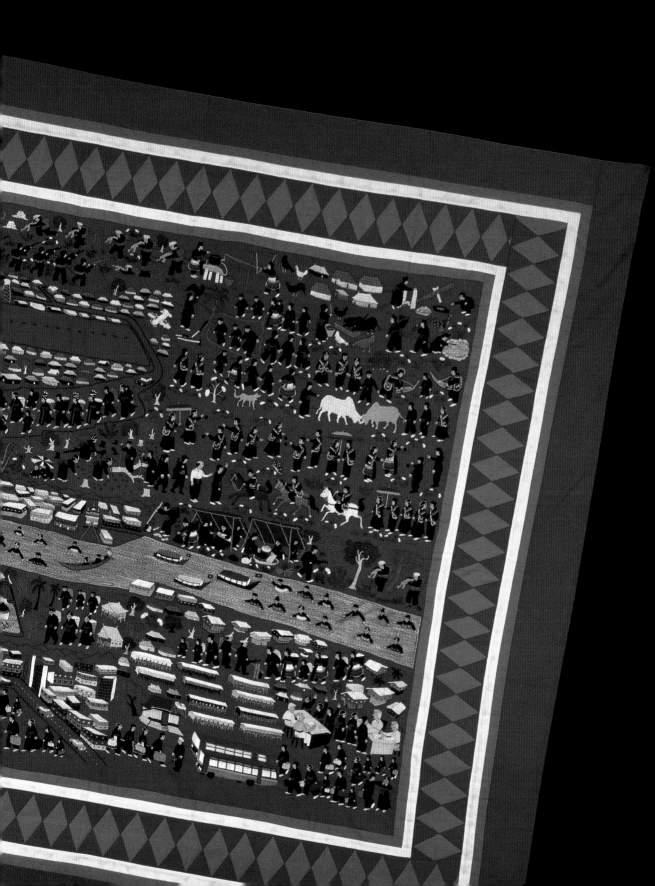

Sept 2ᵈ
1912

Friend Harry
 I recived your letter
also picture of gun and red cote with sketch of old time
saddle and am much obliged
will be in your camp saterdy and we will talk it over
as a talker I am better than a green hand
but with the pen I am Dam ware deaf and dumb
 with regards to you and yours
 Your friend
 C M Russell

PREFACE

What best befits a star? A home full of things, now open to the multitudes of fans who always wondered about the private space of the public figure—a Graceland—a Pickfair—William S. Hart's ranch, or Will Rogers' home?

How about something different—something grand and more serious, a museum providing context for a star's fame—for why a star shone brightly in the West? A museum that would illuminate the whole terrain?

The Autry Museum of Western Heritage is ten years old in 1998. However it is displayed, the context for a collection like the Autry's, rich in popular imagery and material culture, is never linear. Like the heritage it celebrates, it defies boundaries. Consequently, I have conceived my essay to be loose-jointed and free-floating in time as well as space, allusive and elliptical, a meander rather than a race. I have used Charles M. Russell for continuity and as a tour guide through the realm of Western myth.

I appreciate the honor the staff of the Autry Museum of Western Heritage have extended me in asking me to write the essay for a book marking the museum's tenth anniversary, and in granting me the freedom to pursue this project according to my lights. It means that the responsibility for errors in fact or interpretation are mine alone. I regret the errors in fact, but I stand by my interpretations—provisionally, of course.

Two things have inspired me while I worked on this extended essay. One is a framed print of a painting by Peter Hurd, *The Eve of St. John*, that hangs comfortably close to my word processor. I love this painting because one quarter of it is empty. Why is one quarter of it empty? Because the West is spacious, and a racing rider has room to roam.

My other inspiration has been the remark directed to Molly Stark Wood when she shows her great-aunt in Bennington, Vermont, a photograph of the Virginian "in all his cow-boy trappings,—the leathern chaps, the belt and pistol, and in his hand a coil of rope." "My dear," the aunt says, "you have fallen in love with his clothes."

Thanks, as always, to my ever-patient family. I have taxed them this time, but I treasure their love. This book is for Donna, Blake, Scott and my father, Thomas Louvain Dippie.

BRIAN W. DIPPIE

VICTORIA, BRITISH COLUMBIA

How the pink-hued morning clouds
      Go sailing into the west!
And the pearl-white breath of noon,
Or the mists round the silver moon,
  In silent, sheeny crowds
      Go sailing into the west!

WEST

DEFINITIONS

On a warm March day in 1924, Charles M. Russell found himself in Los Angeles riding in an automobile driven by Harry Carey, a member of American royalty at a time when the cowboy was king on the silver screen. It had been a hard past six months for Russell, Montana's nationally-famous Cowboy Artist. The brave appearance he made in Stetson, bright-colored sash around his waist and cowboy boots had failed to stave off the infirmities of age, and he had spent the previous fall bedridden in Great Falls by a crippling attack of sciatica. On March 19 he would turn sixty years old. Perhaps it was just as well that he always got his birth year wrong and believed he was born in 1865. Turning fifty-nine would be less stressful, given he had "been near enough Hell to smell smoke." What since 1920 had been an annual spring vacation in California for the Russells by 1924 was taking on

The glowing, fire-eyed sun
      In glory dies in the west;
And the bird with dreamy crest,
And soft, sun-loving breast,
  When throbbing day is done,
      Floats slowly into the west.

      Oh, everything lovely and fair
            Is floating into the west.
   Tis an unknown land,
                  where our hopes must go,
   And all things beautiful, fluttering slow;
   Our joys all wait for us there,—
            Far out in the dim blue west.[1]

WARD!

the characteristics of something much more. It was their fifth extended stay in "the birth place of Bunko and bungiloos," and Charlie's wife of twenty-seven years and his full-time business manager for most of that time, Nancy Cooper Russell, was angling to move there permanently; just the year before she had purchased a lot in Pasadena next to her father's home, "a white plaster place of Spanish type."[2]

The prospect of moving distressed Charlie Russell. "It is a pritty country this Califonia but I still like home the best," he wrote an artist friend that May. Nancy might pass off her purchase as an investment —indeed, by 1924 the lot had increased in value $900. But, tellingly, she did not sell it and take the profit—and Russell must have seen the writing on a Spanish-type wall of his own. His loyalties were to log-cabin Montana, and they were deep-rooted and unchanging. He'll do to tie-to was the code of the range, and a maxim Russell lived by. Present-day Montana was a frustration to him, what with the farmers and the boosters and the sad spectacle of displaced old-timers—Indians begging for food and hunting scraps from the garbage dumps on the edge of town, and once-hardy cowboys down-and-out in cities like Great Falls, drinking away their remaining days, Prohibition merely adding zest to the challenge of self-destruction. Indeed, Prohibition was just another annoying reminder of how modern moralists had fenced in, then crushed the big-hearted, free-spirited Old West that Russell celebrated in paintings awash in nostalgia. But for all Montana had changed for the worse, it had been home to Charlie Russell since he first lit there in 1880 as a sixteen year old kid fresh from St. Louis, and he would be as stubborn as a Missouri mule when it came to actually moving somewhere else.[3]

Southern California had many advantages. The sunshine and warmth were a relief from Montana's hard winters, and good for old bones and stiff joints. Though Russell groused about the overselling of the Golden State's climate, and claimed that sunshine in California was like near beer—"it looks good thats all"—he had to admit that Montana's winters could be long and unrelenting. Of course, California's boosters put even Montana's to shame, and Russell's acquaintance Irvin S. Cobb, the Sage of Paducah, expressed Russell's sentiments exactly when he wrote:

> "Once upon a time a stranger went to Southern Calfiornia; and when he was asked the customary question—to wit: How do you like the climate?" he said: "No, I don't like it!" So they destroyed him on the spot. I have forgotten now whether they merely hanged him on the nearest tree or burned him at the stake; but they destroyed him utterly and hid his bones in an unmarked grave.

Nevertheless, California's climate was instrumental in the mounting pressure on Russell to move. Nancy, aided by medical advice and Charlie's worsening goiter condition, could employ it like a clamp to squeeze him into compliance.[4]

Russell had many misgivings. He was not quite convinced that California was even part of the West. There was the old suspicion that the Forty-niners in their frenzy to find gold had overlept the "picture and story" part of America—the real West—establishing an East Coast replica on the West Coast that, as a base for subsequent mining rushes, had destroyed the appealing notion of a great wave of settlement rolling magisterially westward by creating countercurrents northward and eastward into, of all things, Charlie Russell's real West! Since the gold rush, California had been an anomaly, its population out of all proportion to that of the other Western states. In the early twentieth century it experienced another transformation as a land boom in Southern California shifted its population locus from the Bay Area to a burgeoning greater Los Angeles. "I think in early days it was a picture country before the boosters made real estate out of it," Russell wrote from Pasadena during his first extended stay in Southern California, "but Im about 100 years late . . . if I was painting frute flowers automobils are [or] flying mashines this would be a good country but nature aint lived here for a long time and thats the old lady Im looking for." Nature defined the real West.[5]

Forty-four years later Wallace Stegner, a sophisticated Western iconoclast who taught the likes of Ken Kesey and Larry McMurtry at Stanford University in Palo Alto, agreed with Russell. California, he asserted flatly, "is not part of the West": "It is the sticks I mean when I speak of the West—the last of the sticks—the subregions between the ninety-eighth meridian and the Sierra-Cascades, where patterns of local habit and belief have developed in some isolation where they are clearer, more innocent, less diluted by outside influences, where they are bred into native sons . . ."[6]

Where—What—was the West? No theme was more common to meditations on the subject than transience. For those who believed the West was whatever lay beyond the borders of civilization, it was by definition fleeting, a temporary stage in the grand drama of human progress. "I am eighty-one years of age," Thomas Jefferson wrote from Monticello in 1824,

born where I now live, in the first range of mountains in the interior of our country. And I have observed this march of civilization advancing from the seacoast, passing over us like a cloud of light, increasing our knowledge and improving our condition, insomuch as that we are at this time more advanced in civilization here than the seaports were when I was a boy. And where this progress will stop no one can say. Barbarism has, in the meantime, been receding before the steady step of amelioration; and will in time, I trust, disappear from the earth.

ABOVE
Rob. Vaughn, 1663
Americae Nova Descriptio
Impensis Anae Seile
Ink on paper
Donated by
Security Pacific Bank

Such was the vision vouchsafed the president in office when Louisiana Territory was purchased from France in 1803, adding the vast trans-Mississippi West to the national domain. "The territory acquired, as it includes all the waters of the Missouri and Mississippi, has more than doubled the area of the United States," he wrote at the time, "and the new parts is not inferior to the old in soil, climate, productions and important communications."[7]

Maps from an earlier age when geographical precision was not even in the cards convey in their very vagueness the open-ended possibilities that made westering compelling. Immediately upon acquiring Lousiana Territory, Jefferson began planning for the first of the great exploring expeditions sponsored by the government to determine what, precisely, the country had acquired, and to test the truthfulness of his leap of faith as to the West's potential. Few were better positioned than the patron of Lewis and Clark to ponder the long-term implications of westering. Ingeniously, Jefferson reversed the tide of emigration to make his point: *Let a philosophic observer commence a journey from the savages of the Rocky Mountains, eastwardly towards our seacoast. These he would observe in the earliest state of association living under no law but that of nature, subsisting and covering themselves with the flesh and skins of wild beasts. He would next find those on our frontiers in the pastoral state, raising domestic animals to supply the defects of hunting. Then succeed our own semi-barbarous citizens, the pioneers of the advance of civilization, and so in his progress he would meet the gradual shades of improving man until he would reach his, as yet, most improved state in our seaport towns. This, in fact, is equivalent to a survey, in time, of the progress of man from the infancy of creation to the present day.* The West was where the East was not.

LEFT
Bryant Baker
The Pioneer Woman, 1927
Gorham Company Founders,
casting number 12
Bronze

The completion of the Pacific Railroad in 1869 was another milestone in the opening of the West that occasioned self-conscious commemoration, and a slew of travel books trumpeting the scenic wonders awaiting the tourist who would make the trip to California. George Pine employed an appropriately bookish metaphor in the preface to his contribution to the literature, *Beyond the West; Containing an Account of Two Years' Travel in that Other Half of Our Great Continent Far Beyond The Old West, on the Plains, in the Rocky Mountains, and Picturesque Parks of Colorado* (1870):

> Twenty odd years ago, little was known of that somewhat mysterious part of our continent, lying far beyond our ideas of the Old West, except as the far-off land of the Indian, the hunter and trapper, the furs and the home of the buffalo. One great blank book—mostly without a preface—with a few scratches here and there only, on the title page. But how diligently and understandingly the types were made, set up and electrotyped, within a few years past. We see the now unabridged edition, bound in a style more useful than ornamental, (not yet gilt edged,) but nicely sprinkled and held together with the great civilizer—iron rails.

Pine went on to explain the plethora of Wests—including the title page allusions to "The Sunset Land, California the End of the West"—in a chapter called "Where Is the West?":

> Chicago is no longer western, but is an eastern city. It is only 900 miles to the Atlantic coast, while it is 2,350 miles to the Pacific coast. Dividing the Union into east, centre and west, the eastern division will embrace all the States lying east of the Mississippi river; the central, all the States and Territories between the Mississippi and the Rocky Mountains; and the western, all the States and Territories between the Rocky Mountains and the Pacific coast . . . . The completion of the Pacific Railway has changed the central, and moved the west 1,200 miles toward the setting sun. The actual west consists of California, Oregon, Washington, Nevada, Arizona, Utah, Montana, Wyoming, and the major portion of Colorado and New Mexico. It is hard to realize the truth that Chicago is an eastern city, and that Illinois is not even a central, but is an eastern state. Omaha, which has always been regarded as on the western verge of the 'Far West,' is in fact 150 miles east of the center of the Union! Consequently, we can with propriety style this book Beyond the Old West.[8]

When Theodore Roosevelt, who would occupy the White House exactly a century after Jefferson, began writing a multi-volume history of *The Winning of the West* in the late 1880s, he intended to be Francis Parkman's successor. Parkman, to whom Roosevelt dedicated his work, had narrated the long French-English struggle for mastery in North America; Roosevelt picked up the narrative thread in 1763, and provided the half-century sequel. His title referred to the winning of the trans-Allegheny west, not the trans-Mississippi West. Indeed, when, in 1896, he finally reached the nineteenth century and the government-sponsored explorations of the Louisiana Purchase that closed the fourth and final volume of his history, he was left to redefine his topic: "The Far West, the West beyond the Mississippi, had been thrust on

Jefferson, and given to the nation, by the rapid growth of the Old West, the West that lay between the Alleghenies and the Mississippi." Wests to the left of them, Wests to the right of them, into the valley of semantic confusion rode the bold writers![9]

Such geographic hairsplitting was unnecessary. Where was the seat of the romance, the epic challenge? There, at any given moment, was the West! Despairing of finding any physical frontier—"Go where we will on the surface of things, men have been there before us"—Henry David Thoreau concluded, "The frontiers are not east or west, north or south, but wherever a man fronts a fact." This corresponds to the observation that "America was Europe's 'West' before it was America." Beginning points are as elusive as frontiers: the West is forever in flight. "And where is its location?" George Catlin asked in the 1830s: "phantom-like it flies before us as we travel, and on our way is continually gilded, before us, as we approach the setting sun." The West has the quality of dream about it, a fitful dream in which the dreamer tries to keep up with someone or something. Legs stretch out and out, but while ground is covered the trunk remains stationary as the object of desire recedes into the distance. If the West is a dreamland, it is a land of fevered dreams.[10]

"AND ONE FINE MORNING—"

In 1925 F. Scott Fitzgerald published *The Great Gatsby*, "a story of the West, after all," in which a self-invented dreamer going by the name Jay Gatsby, inspired in turn by an earlier dreamer named Dan Cody whose fortune came from "every rush for metal" in the West since 1875, clings desperately to the belief that you can repeat the past. But the East has proven impervious to West-dreaming parvenus, and the story's narrator is left to reflect sadly on the exhaustion of the American Dream:

> *I became aware of the old island here that flowered once for Dutch sailors' eyes—a fresh, green breast of the new world. Its vanished trees, the trees that had made way for Gatsby's house, had once pandered in whispers to the last and rarest of all human dreams; for a transitory enchanted moment man must have held his breath in the presence of this continent, compelled into an aesthetic contemplation he neither understood nor desired, face to face for the last time in history with something commensurate to his capacity for wonder . . . .*
>
> *Gatsby believed in . . . the orgiastic future that year by year recedes before us. It eluded us then, but that's no matter—tomorrow we will run faster, stretch out our arms farther . . . .*
> *And one fine morning—*[11]

"West-fever," O. E. Rolvaag called it, and it has left an impression on American literature
as pronounced as the first furrow on an unbroken plain. "People drifted about in a sort of
delirium, like sea birds in mating time," Rolvaag wrote in *Giants in the Earth* (1927), "then
they flew toward the sunset, in small flocks and large—always toward Sunset Land . . . .
here on the trackless plains, the thousand-year hunger of the poor after human happiness
had been unloosed!" In the end, the dream consumes the dreamers. Rolvaag's protagonist,
sent into a raging winter blizzard, never returns. But in the spring his body is found,
seated on the west side of a haystack, the face "ashen and drawn. His eyes were set
toward the west."[12]

"The history of every country begins in the heart of a man or a woman,"
Willa Cather observed in *O Pioneers!* (1913). Thus a pioneer must be a dreamer,
"able to enjoy the idea of things more than the things themselves." Cather's
West-dreamer is Alexanda Bergson, an independent version of the pioneer
mother honored in monuments across the West: it is to the land that she is
married. Finally resigned to accepting the conventional role of a man's wife,
"She was still gazing into the west, and in her face there was that exalted
serenity that sometimes came to her at moments of deep feeling. The
level rays of the sinking sun shone in her clear eyes."[13]

"Where is home?" Wallace Stegner asked of one of his characters
driving west in June in the middle of the Depression:

> The whole nation had been footloose too long. Heaven had been just
> over the next range for too many generations. Why remain in one
> dull plot of earth when Heaven was reachable, was touchable, was
> just over there? . . .
>
> Was he going home, or just to another place? . . . He had a notion where home
> would turn out to be, for himself as for his father—over the next range, on the Big Rock Candy
> Mountain, that place of impossible loveliness that had pulled the whole nation westward, the place where
> the fat land sweated up wealth and the heavens dropped lemonade . . .
>
> He looked up the straight road running clean and white westward between elms and wild plum
> thickets . . . The sky to the west was a clear blue . . .

The West forever shining in the eyes of the dreamer, a whole nation "footloose too long." Told that
"A man can't just traipse on forever," Dick Summers, the veteran mountain man who has guided a party
of settlers to Oregon in A. B. Guthrie, Jr.'s *The Way West* (1949), ponders the point, then replies: "After a
while he meets the ocean, Lije."[14]

ABOVE
Colt Model 1851 Navy Revolver
.36 caliber, ivory grips with carved eagle motif, serial #138824
Backstrap reads "J.B. Hickok, 1869."
This Model 1851 Colt Navy Revolver was one of a pair presented
to James Butler "Wild Bill" Hickok in 1869 upon his election as
Marshall of Hays City, Kansas. It is engraved in the style of the
Colt factory's famous engraver Gustave Young. The holster dates
to ca. 1870. Hickok was murdered while playing cards in a
Deadwood, South Dakota saloon in 1876. He died holding two
black eights and a pair of black aces, the "Dead Man's Hand."

Questing: the journey rather than the destination. It is the refrain in Cormac McCarthy's astonishing postmodern exegisis of Western violence, *Blood Meridian; Or the Evening Redness in the West* (1985), where the metaphor of riding on is rendered horrific by his company of mercenaries' scourging the Southwestern border in search of scalps, and wallowing in blood. There are no hopeful dreamers in this land; even the gold-seekers streaming to California are simply "itinerant degenerates bleeding westward like some heliotropic plague." But for all their compulsive, shark-like violence, McCarthy's scalp-hunters resemble the starry-eyed pioneers of Western myth in one respect: they, too, "run plumb out of country" and end up on the Pacific shore, staring out to sea "while the sun dipped hissing in the swells." By night only a riderless horse is left, motionless at last, "watching, out there past men's knowing, where the stars are drowning and whales ferry their vast souls through the black and seamless sea."[15]

Movement in Larry McMurtry's *Lonesome Dove* (1985) is towards a more human resolution. A trail drive from Texas to Montana serves as the basis for a picaresque tale that balances violence with humor in telling the story of two old friends who "had roved too long"—former Texas Rangers Gus McCrae and Woodrow F. Call, "people of the horse, not of the town." From Lonesome Dove, Texas, they set out north to a new promised land. McCrae is a realist with the flair of a poet. "The earth is mostly just a boneyard," he explains, adding, "But pretty in the sunlight." McCrae meets his end in Montana. Fleeing from attacking Indians, he suffers arrow wounds in both legs. He manages to reach Miles City, where one leg is amputated. His roving days are done. "Look there at Montana," he tells his partner as he stares out the window from his deathbed. "It's fine and fresh, and now we've come and it'll soon be ruint, like my legs."[16]

We continually hear echoes in Western prose. McCarthy's coda recalls John Steinbeck's conclusion to *The Red Pony* (1937), while McCrae's final soliloquy evokes Boone Caudill's recognition of the self-destructive nature of westering in A.B. Guthrie's *The Big Sky* (1947). "It was westering and westering," the loquacious grandfather in *The Red Pony* muses, trying to explain to his grandson Jody the irresistible power westering exerted, and the crushing disappointment when it ended:

"We carried life out here and set it down the way those ants carry eggs. And I was the leader. The westering was as big as God, and the slow steps that made the movement piled up until the continent was crossed.

"Then we came down to the sea, and it was done."

So the grandfather sits in his chair on a porch above the Pacific, one in "a line of old men along the shore hating the ocean because it stopped them." In *The Big Sky*, the same vedict is rendered by a taciturn mountain man who can only sense the shrinking of space and hope. "It's all sp'iled, I reckon, Dick," Boone tells his mountain man partner, "The whole caboodle."[17]

Westering delivered successive eulogies. When Woodrow Call returned to Lonesome Dove after burying Gus McCrae, "the harsh clanging of the dinner bell . . . made him feel that he rode through a land of ghosts. He felt lost in his mind and wondered if all the boys would be there when he got home."

The year before he died, Charlie Russell painted a night scene, an exercise in purest nostalgia, titled *Laugh Kills Lonesome* (1925). It showed a wrangler stepping into the circle of light to join a group of grinning cowboys seated around the campfire. That wrangler was Russell himself, rejoining his compadres of forty years past. "My me[m]ory often takes me back to the range, and camps we knew so well," he wrote one of his few surviving cowboy friends in 1917. "Theres not maney of the old bunch left. right now I know more dead men than live ones, and if you count back youl find its the same with you. thirty seven years Iv lived in Montana, but Im among strangers now."[18] You could still live in Montana, but the real Montana was gone. "We got no kick coming," Russell wrote "Teddy Blue" Abbott, an old-timer who had trailed cattle north from Texas to Montana, "we got the cream." A few months before he died, Russell elaborated in a letter to Charlie Beil, one of the new generation of cowboy artists who, inspired by his example, would keep his West alive after he was gone: "When I came west I got the cream let the come lattys have the skim milk." Charlie Russell's Montana, like all the Old West, was not just a place; it was a place in time.[19]

Below
Buckskin Suit, Hat and Shooting Glasses
Worn by "Antelope"
Ernst Bauman, ca. 1875

A Place in Time, and Buckskin Bravery

Eastering from California to Montana was a hard dose to swallow for a regional loyalist like Charlie Russell, who always thought of Montana as the real Old West. But he recognized the legacy of older cowboy cultures on his beloved Montana range—cowboy lingo and gear and techniques bearing the unmistakable stamp of California and Texas. "By all I can find out from old, gray headed punchers, the cow business started in California, 'n the Spaniards were the first to burn marks on their cattle 'n hosses, 'n use the rope," he wrote in "The Story of the Cowboy," published in 1916. "Then men from the States drifted west to Texas, pickin' up the brandin' iron 'n lass-rope, 'n the business spread north, east 'n west, till the spotted longhorns walked in every trail marked out by their brown cousins—the buffalo." This made Montana a come-lately when it came to cowboying—come lately being Russell's favorite put-down for the boosters who had swarmed into Montana after he arrived as a sixteen year old fresh from St. Louis just in time to catch the tail end of his Old West. And that is the point. Since the West was Catlin's phantom, always over the next horizon, it was not a place at all, but a moment in time, evanescent, glorious —and gone forever, as Theodore Roosevelt, erstwhile Dakota rancher, would write in his autobiography in 1913, "'gone, gone with lost Atlantis,' gone to the isle of ghosts and of strange dead memories."[20]

Russell had embraced one version of the West in Montana, then. But since it was the final version —or so the artists and writers of his generation contended in elegiac paintings and prose—it had to represent the last best West, the Far West of Pine and Roosevelt, now fixed forever in time and place. Roosevelt's *Winning of the West* found shelf-space in Russell's library. Boyhood reading about Daniel Boone, Davy Crockett, Kit Carson and the rest of that buckskin brigade that wended its way through American history had first kindled his enthusiasm for the West. In a sketchbook dating from 1879, the year before he went to Montana, he drew the panoply of frontier types that filled his imagination—war-painted Indians, miners gingerly picking their way down rocky precipices, and trappers chasing and being chased by man and animal. Cowboys (apart from a few Mexican *vaqueros*) did not enter the equation at this early date because they were not yet indelibly imprinted on the landscape of the popular imagination. Instead, men in buckskins predominated, and bears (bears galore—hand-to-hand encounters were a staple of early Western art) and wolves and dense forests—the stuff of America's epic when the frontier still conjured up images of the heroic age of Daniel Boone and Kentucky's dark and bloody ground. In going to Montana, young Charlie Russell hoped to catch a glimpse of a passing caravan.[21]

There were bound to be pockets of the West where the horizon was still uncluttered and with ample room for dreaming. On the last page of his sketchbook, Russell drew a careful pencil portrait of "Bufalow Bill The American Scout." He showed him in full buckskins, fringed and beaded, his handsome features and flowing hair framed by the sweeping brim of his hat. For Russell's generation, William F. "Buffalo Bill" Cody personified the frontier ideal. Rugged and manly, and already the hero in a series of fictitious dime novel adventures, he had drawn on his fame as a buffalo hunter and scout and Indian-fighter to great effect through the 1870s in stage plays anticipating the arena entertainment that, beginning in 1883, would make him America's greatest showman, Buffalo Bill's Wild West. William F. Cody only had one role, and that was Buffalo Bill. When he killed the Cheyenne Yellow Hair on July 17, 1876 and took the "First scalp for Custer" he "became more than real," Paul Fees has written, "he became part of the myth of the West." An impressionable boy like Russell took his cues from Buffalo Bill: the days of Boone and Crockett and Carson were not done yet. But you had to get "out there" soon, before the railroad and settlers and fences hemmed it all in and wrecked the West forever.[22]

Russell turned sixteen in March 1880, and his parents finally yielded to his importuning: he could go to Montana and join a family friend there for a spell. The assumption, of course, was that reality would knock the romance out of his head, and he would return to St. Louis a chastened young man prepared to get on with the serious business of life. But it was the heart, not the head, that nourished romance. The setting sun lit up the land and rekindled boyhood dreams. Look hard enough with eyes filled with that Western light and fantasies could still find form. If the Indians in Montana in 1880 were not very wild, and if the buffalo herds that once carpeted the plains were down to a pitiful remnant and buffalo hunts a thing of the past, one could read back from what was to what used to be. And if the days of mountain men were just a memory, one could still put on a buckskin jacket, roam with a professional hunter named Jake Hoover in the remote Judith Basin, and play at being "Bufalow Bill The American Scout." "To me, a boy lately from the east," Russell recalled, "riding by Jake's side through a country like this seemed like a chapter from one of my favorite romances of the Rocky Mountains."[23]

Russell chose to see Buffalo Bill as a romantic figure from the past. In fact, Buffalo Bill represented both a heroic yesterday and a progressive tomorrow. He was in the vanguard of change; his legendary deeds paved the way for future development. He was Boone Caudill, spoiling what he loved, but unlike Jody's grandfather in *The Red Pony*, he had no regrets. He was why the West fled phantom-like before the seeker. Where he went, it was no more. Cody personified the myth of the winning of the West—a unifying myth for post-Civil War America, as Fees has observed, "with its celebration of individual heroic values and collective national accomplishment." Cody stood for progress, but he was a throwback in appearance—and appearance was everything. Until the cowboy displaced the frontiersman in the affections of the public, buckskins signified the Western hero.[24]

John Wallace "Captain Jack" Crawford, who also scouted in the Sioux War of 1876, performed on stage with Cody before launching a solo career with a gimmick of his own. Captain Jack was the clean-living "Poet Scout," otherwise, he was a Cody clone. They all were—all the frontier heroes who tromped the stage and preened for the camera like modern rock stars. Hats invariably set at a rakish angle, heads tilted to show the features to best advantage, long hair falling to the shoulders, a silk kerchief loosely knotted around the neck, they exude a cocksure confidence endearing in its vanity. Even the relatively dour James Butler Hickok got into the spirit of things during his brief stint on the stage with Buffalo Bill, donned buckskins and looked fully the part of "Wild Bill," celebrated Western gunfighter.[25]

The progression is essentially linear when tracing an actual person or event through various forms of popular culture to, say, a cinematic portrayal where the star's persona melds with that of the historical figure (Errol Flynn as George Armstrong Custer, Paul Newman as

ABOVE
Apache-made Buckskin Shirt
Worn by a U.S. soldier in Southwestern campaigns and the Red River War of 1874.

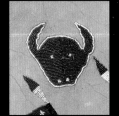

Buckskin Jacket
Worn by William F. "Buffalo Bill" Cody
Buckskin with beadwork decoration, ca. 1900
Acquisition made possible in part John E. Bianchi Jr.

Buffalo Bill Cody). But the progression is loopy when the actual figure (Buffalo Bill) portrays himself performing an actual deed. Things get especially interesting when the historical figure, prior to performing the deed or even while performing it, has his eyes fixed on how it will "play" after the fact. On the day Buffalo Bill killed and scalped Yellow Hair, he was wearing a stage costume chosen for the occasion. His motivation: when he returned to the stage that fall, he could truthfully claim that the costume his audience was seeing was just like the one he wore when he took the first scalp for Custer. Art imitating life imitating art.[26]

What does it mean to wear an authentic outfit in a completely impausible melodrama based on real events? Buffalo Bill could display the actual scalp he took from Yellow Hair to affirm his credentials as an Indian-fighting scout. Wild Bill fell to an assassin's bullet while playing poker in Deadwood in 1876; no one could challenge his credentials as a "prince of pistoleers." Other would-be Western heroes had little more to offer their audiences in the way of credentials than a buckskin suit, and fancy buckskins were a dead giveaway if you were anyone other than Buffalo Bill. "Antelope" Ernst Bauman hit upon an ingenious solution. His stage costume was a buckskin outfit tailor-made about 1878 in emulation of Cody and the rest, and actually worn during his career as a buffalo hunter. The suit is not picturesquely bedaubed: it is filthy, with spatters on the sleeves and grimy fringe. On stage, these buckskins were an immaculate credential, proof positive that "Antelope" was no Western pretender, but the real McCoy.

The temptation is strong to view buckskins in whatever form as fraudulent, and their wearers as showmen or poseurs. But this is to replicate the postmodernist's error of denying any reality in order to expose constructed realities. Push against the buckskin construct, and behind it is what was. Plains Indian men wore loose-fitting hide shirts, and whites who moved among them in the nineteenth century were quick to follow suit, from fur trappers to soldiers serving in the frontier army. Recounting his hunting experiences in the vicinity of Forts Union and Berthold in the years 1847-48, the English sportsman John Palliser recommended Scottish woollens over leather which, "after all, is but an inconvenient substitute . . . ; for though it has its advantages in point of wear, it is horribly uncomfortable in wet weather, and dries as hard and stiff as parchment." However, when his woolen shooting-coat "was completely worn out," Palliser spent three days fashioning a well-dressed elkskin "into a hunting-shirt with loose sleeves, sewing it up partly with buffalo sinew and partly with thread . . .; the dressed skin of a small deer furnished the pockets in front . . . I found this a most effective hunting shirt for no brushwood could tear it." He also made himself a pair of deer-hide leggins, and upon his return to Fort Union had his hunting-shirt ornamented by Crow women "on the breast, and along the sleeves, with the most brilliant porcupine-work edged with blue glass beads." Adaptation as well as affectation played a role in the buckskin ethos.[27]

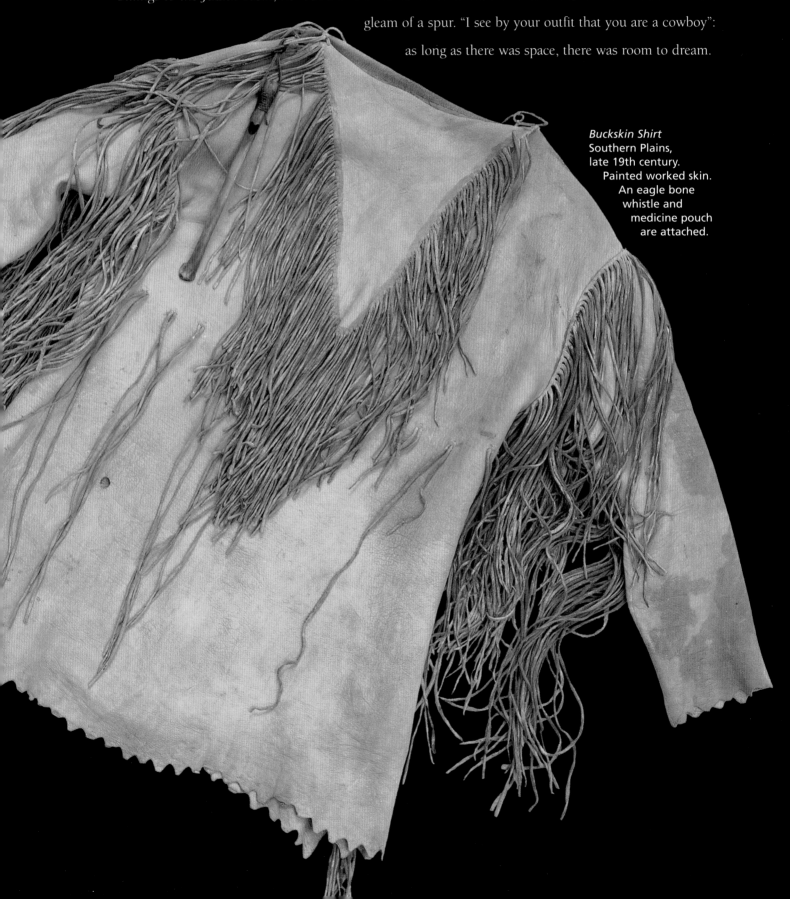

Since he carried so much baggage with him and looked for what conformed to his expectations, Russell knew that he was riding drag, not point, when it came to westering. But Montana offered him his own place in time, a West defined by what he thought the West should be. For one year he accompanied Jake Hoover, living out his buckskin fantasies, and then, signalling his transition from trapper to cowboy, the Buckskin Kid, as he was known, became Kid Russell. Hired on to tend horses on a cattle drive from Billings to the Judith Basin, he found a new variation on an old romance in the flash of a Stetson and the gleam of a spur. "I see by your outfit that you are a cowboy": as long as there was space, there was room to dream.

Buckskin Shirt
Southern Plains,
late 19th century.
Painted worked skin.
An eagle bone
whistle and
medicine pouch
are attached.

ROOM TO ROAM: SPACE AND THE WESTERN HERO

Western space was not a neutral condition. It was the first "fact" everyone had to "front." And representing that space remained a formidable artistic challenge. How do you make emptiness visually interesting? The act of writing, Wayne Fields has observed, is a horizontal exercise; words appeal to the inner eye, and thus are better suited than the visual arts to the task of portraying what is not there. Listen to Willa Cather paint a word picture in *My Antonia*:

> North of the house, inside the ploughed fire-breaks, grew a thick-set strip of box-elder trees, low and bushy, their leaves already turning yellow. This hedge was nearly a quarter of a mile long, but I had to look very hard to see it at all. The little trees were insignificant against the grass. It seemed as if the grass were about to run over them, and over the plum-patch behind the sod chicken-house.
>
> As I looked about me I felt that the grass was the country, as the water is the sea . . . . more than anything else I felt motion in the landscape; in the fresh, easy-blowing morning wind, and in the earth itself, as if the shaggy grass were a sort of loose hide, and underneath it herds of wild buffalo were galloping, galloping . . . . . . I wanted to walk straight on through the red grass and over the edge of the world, which could not be very far away. The light air about me told me that the world ended here: only the ground and sun and sky were left, and if one went a little farther there would be only sun and sky, and one would float off into them, like the tawny hawks which sailed over our heads making slow shadows on the grass.[28]

Writers can describe desert or plains in terms of absence; painting, in contrast, achieves its effect through what it can show, through what is there to be seen. Earlier frontiers yielded the potent metaphor of the clearing in the forest to symbolize civilized advance in America: the woods represented a waste and howling wilderness, the clearing literally enlightenment as sunshine spilled onto soil rescued from eternal darkness. Tree stumps traced the march of pioneering progress in a land redeemed by the axe and made fruitful for the plow. What would be an equivalent prairie metaphor for change? Progress had made the vertical horizontal in the woodlands; the flatlands would undergo no comparable transformation to catch the artist's eye. The plow turning the prairie sod, the first furrow on the plains. These marked the advent of agrarian civilization in the face of the "annihilating power of emptiness."[29]

The artists who accompanied the official exploring expeditions before the Civil War, trained as they were in topographical draftsmanship, were up to the task of reporting back on the land and its potential. They were receptive to panoramic renderings without important human presence. The Eastern

press, especially after the completion of the transcontinental railroad in 1869, wanted something different: the human drama on the Western borders. Illustrators provided it, naturally concentrating on the sensational, the Wild West. With people front and center, the effect can be claustrophobic: a cramped, pinched vision of life in the frontier towns. Judging from the illustrated papers, the West was one giant saloon, gambling den and brothel. There were shoot-outs and cut-ups galore, but no breathing room.[30]

Wide-open space and the opportunity it connoted had brought those townsfolk west in the first place. But how to portray it? The prairie was a stand-in for infinity. One could join Snake in the Grass, the subject of an 1868 painting by John Mix Stanley, in a reverie that touched on the meaning of life. "I often landed my skiff and mounted the green carpeted bluffs, whose soft grassy tops, invited me to recline, where I was at once lost in contemplation," George Catlin, the most visionary of Western artists, wrote of his travels on the upper Missouri in 1832:

> Soul melting scenery that was about me! . . . even the soft
> tones of sweet music would scarcely preserve a spark to light
> the soul again, that had passed this sweet delirium. I mean
> the prairie, whose enamelled plains that lie beneath me, in
> distance soften into . . . sweetness like an essence . . . I mean
> this prairie; where Heaven sheds its purest light and lends
> its richest tints . . .

One could join Catlin on a buffalo hunt, a staple of Western art that took full advantage of horizontal space, mirroring his perception of the West as "a vast country of green fields, where the men are all red." Or one could join those less romantically-inclined who despaired of ever crossing that desolate, forlorn, unvarying stretch of prairie land. The classic comparison likened the prairie to the ocean—the wind rippling the tall grass and the shadows created by scudding clouds resembled the swell of the sea. One needed verticals to render the sight meaningful. The ship's mast riding the waves provided a human scale for gauging immensity; the prairies provided none. "The eternal illimitable sweep of the undulating prairie" oppressed a traveler in the 1840s with "a sense of vastness quite over-whelming." Prairie optics, abetted by the dry clear air, were confusing: "The eye ranges over a sea of short waving grass without a single intervening object to afford it the accustomed means of estimating relative size and distance."[31]

In 1858 Humphrey L. Hime, who served as photographer with the Assiniboine and Saskatchewan Exploring Expedition sent out to survey the future Canadian west, made a memorable view with a title as direct as the image itself: *The Prairie looking west*. Hime met the challenge of the absolutely flat horizon line by including in his image one bone and, dead center in the foreground, a human skull. Absence had to be enlivened with something. But in another view, Hime offered an uncompromising image of emptiness. Titled *The Prairie, on the banks of the Red River, looking south* it offers no verticals at all; instead a trail crosses the foreground in perfect parallel to the horizon line. Everything is flat, the overpowering fact of Western space the only message. As Willa Cather wryly observed: "The only thing very noticeable about Nebraska was that it was still, all day long, Nebraska."[32]

Coming to terms with space was every Western artist's challenge. It took time to penetrate artistic convention. Thomas Moran spent a career repenting an uninformed illustration for *Scribner's Monthly* in 1871 that turned the Grand Canyon of the Yellowstone into a narrow chasm "about four feet wide and four miles deep," Wallace Stegner commented, bearing no resemblance to nature's panoramic grandeur. The dazzling breadth of the view defied the landscape painter's fondness for compressing sprawling reality within the confines of a canvas by hedging the view with trees or rocky crags on either side. Moran had never been west of Michigan when he undertook his *Scribner's* assignment; upon seeing the Yellowstone for himself later that same year, he expanded on convention to accommodate spacious Western reality in a mammoth oil seven feet high and ten feet wide, *The Grand Canyon of the Yellowstone* (1872).[33]

When it came to such mountain grandeur, the painter had the edge over the writer: words that could take the measure of the plains were inadequate to convey the sensational—that is, the sensation mountain scenery inspired in the beholder. Albert Bierstadt, in a career full of commercial calculation, dazzled the public with Western vistas that were dreams made tangible. He traveled the West in 1859, and *Landscape with Indians*, a painting done at the time, has a refreshing, unforced quality; his patented effects, the basis of his huge popular reputation in the 1860s and '70s, are more evident in oils like *Sunset on the Plains* and, particularly, *Mountain Lake*. Its theatricality is pure Bierstadt; but it could not hope to match Moran's 1875 masterpiece *Mountain of the Holy Cross*. Using every trick in the artist's book, rearranging nature at will, Moran created a soaring landscape that allows the eye to trail up a rushing, tumbling mountain stream, through a sunlit valley and low-lying cloud shrouding the mountain's base to confront like a revelation the majestic peak with its cross outlined in snow. It is an emotional trip that the eye takes to the summit, expressing the overpowering sensation of the sublime. Technique and message fuse. God smiles on America.[34]

All two-dimensional representations have borders—and while artists have pushed against them, rendering the wonders of the Grand Canyon, for example, in a triptych, there is a final border left and right, and a ceiling on the sky. Western art has struggled to suggest the limitless within limits that are both literal and metaphorical. The lofty skyscapes of Maynard Dixon come to mind. They dwarf human endeavor, the ant-like frenzy that impelled Jody's grandfather to carry life to the Pacific shore. (On the

ABOVE
Thomas W. Whittredge (1820-1910)
The Little Blue River, ca. 1865
Oil on cardboard

BELOW
Albert Bierstadt (1830-1902)
Landscape with Indians, ca. 1859
Oil on panel

movie screen, in contrast, the hero stands all the
taller against that towering sky, the sole vertical
in a horizontal world.) Three-dimensional
works provide another solution to the problem
of portraying Western space. Sculpture's freeing
of the form from context strongly appealed to
Frederic Remington, the most influential Western
illustrator of the late nineteenth century.
Unhappy in his craft, tired of illustrating the
words of others for black and white reproduction,
he yearned to become a pure painter, to work
freely within his chosen repertoire of Western

subjects and, for that matter, to paint landscapes out of doors. His Western oils—the "Grand Frontier"
as he called them—were studio creations; landscapes, whether done near his summer home on the St.
Lawrence River or on one of his Western excursions, perhaps to serve as background for a major performance piece, invited spontaneity. As a professional illustrator Remington knew
that the figure was everything; as an aspiring artist eager to grapple with
the challenge of conveying the infinite, he had warred with the limits
imposed by paint and canvas. Sculpture set
him free. He had done his share of
paintings in the past showing cowboys
riding bucking horses. But in 1895 he
tried his hand at a new medium, and
the result was a bronze masterpiece,
The Bronco Buster. It fits within an
established illustrative tradition, but as a sculpture
it was unprecedented. Devoid of setting, Remington's horse
and rider are free to occupy any space the imagination desires.[35]

LEFT
Frederic Remington (1861-1909)
The Bronco Buster, 1895
Roman Bronze Works, New York,
Casting Number 26
Bronze
Donated by Mr. and Mrs. Gene Autry

ABOVE
W.H.D. Koerner
*A Bucking Horse of Ability,
1926*
Oil on canvas
*Donated by
Ruth Koerner Oliver*

SMOKE
DAVY CROCKETT
BEST
5¢
CIGAR
"BE SURE YOU'RE RIGHT, THEN GO AHEAD"

Space mattered more than ever to Remington's generation. Since the creation of the Republic, Americans had the benefit of a vast, landed estate to the west. The public domain was a collective legacy. But in 1890 the Superintendent of the Census had proclaimed an end to the "frontier of settlement," and three years later, in his celebrated essay "The Significance of the Frontier in American History," Frederick Jackson Turner had explained the implications of that pronouncement. "Since the days when the fleet of Columbus sailed into the waters of the New World," he wrote, "America has been another name for opportunity." Open land and opportunity had gone together, and the exhaustion of one perhaps foretold the exhaustion of the other. At the least, the closing of the physical frontier checked mobility and, with it, the necessity to continually adapt to new environments. Yet such adaptation was, in Turner's view, the very process that had shaped a distinctive American character combining coarseness and strength, acuteness and inquisitiveness, practicality, inventiveness, materialism, "that restless, nervous energy; that dominant individualism working for good and for evil, and withal that buoyancy and exuberance which comes with freedom."[36]

Historically, individualism in America has received mixed reviews. "Working for good and evil," it has often been perceived as a social threat. How do you govern people who believe they have a God-given right to march to their own drummer? Or who believe in the duty of civil disobedience, and the proposition that "any man more right than his neighbors constitutes a majority of one already"? Davy Crockett's motto, "Be sure you're right, then go ahead," would have brought a stony rebuke from the Puritan Fathers. They had no problem distinguishing between civil liberty, which meant proper social constraints, and natural liberty, which was simply license for corrupt humankind to do wrong. It took time, and a more benign perspective on human nature, for individualism to flourish as a cultural ideal. The classic Western hero remains something of a social misfit. But, attuned to higher natural law, he knows right from wrong instinctively. The arbiter of an uncomplicated justice, he is friend to the virtuous and mortal enemy to wrong-doers. The Western hero resolves the conflict between social responsibility and individual rights by honoring both. And so the community's function is confidently turned over to an individual's conscience in this commemorative tribute to Buffalo Bill Cody:

> Across the rolling, trackless plains
> I see a vision as of old.
> Aye, like a knight in armor girt,
> As noble, free and quite as bold;
> His flowing locks and massive brow
> Proclaimed the gallant life he passed
> While toiling to prepare the way
> For those who built an empire vast.
> They called him Bill—
> Just Buffalo Bill.

> What were the thoughts that filled his brain
> While waiting for the final call?
> Methinks he saw the blood-stained trail,
> The rifles flash, the red man's fall.
> The war-whoop and the massacre.
> Ah, God! His life was one great fight
> To master man and elements,
> To force the erring mortal right.
> They called him Bill—
> Just Buffalo Bill.[37]

The Bronco Buster served another function for Remington's generation. It helped define the moment when the cowboy arrived as the dominant Western hero. Buckskin-clad plainsmen would go on, of course. Buffalo Bill did not die until 1917, and mountain men still have their devoted following. But since the publication of Owen Wister's *The Virginian* in 1902, the cowboy has been king. *The Virginian* was set in Wyoming in the period 1874-90, "a vanished world" that once was home to the horseman of the plains. "But he will never come again," Wister told his readers at the outset. "He rides in his historic yesterday." Nevertheless, as a hero the Virginian was irresistible. A respecter of women and lover of horses, a self-reliant individual with simple virtues and an uncompromising moral code, he "was not more than six feet," but "in his eye, in his face, in his step, in the whole man, there dominated a something potent to be felt, I should think, by man or woman." It might be the case, as Wister said, that "you will no more see him gallop out of the unchanging silence than you will see Columbus on the unchanging sea come sailing from Palos with his caravels." But that only added to his romantic allure. Certainly Molly Stark Wood was smitten:

> No one of her admirers had ever been like this creature. The fringed leathern chaparreros, the cartridge belt, the flannel shirt, the knotted scarf at the neck, these things were now an old story to her. Since her arrival [from Vermont] she had seen young men and old in plenty dressed thus. But worn by this man now standing by her door, they seemed to radiate romance.

A huge best-seller—indeed, the first American novel to sell a million copies—*The Virginian* inspired a stage play, four movies, a television series, a mountain of dubious fiction, and, no doubt, a passel of cowboy wannabes, women as well as men, eager to sample Western life on a dude ranch, sleep under the stars, and knot their own scarf at the neck.[38]

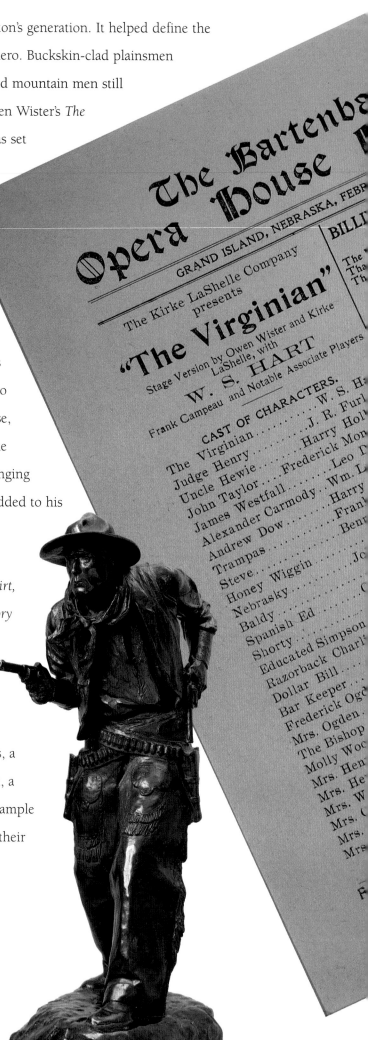

RIGHT
Charles Christadoro
Two Gun Bill (William S. Hart), 1925
Gorham Company Foundry, New York
Bronze

The Virginian adhered to a code of rugged individualism. "Now back East you can be middling and get along," he explained. "But if you go to try a thing on in this Western country, you've got to do it well." You alone were responsible for your actions. Westerns in the first half of the twentieth century consistently espoused the same values as *The Virginian*, and every cowboy hero embodied them. Thus Thomas H. Ince's rules for a William S. Hart Western, laid down in 1918. Hart must win any physical confrontation in which he was involved to keep him "on his cinema pedestal"; he must have the opportunity to demonstate his "superiority as a horseman"; and "he must be pictured as a big-hearted, whole-souled, rough-spoken man with a wealth of real affection for animals, children and womenfolk." Gene Autry's code of proper conduct, set out in his "Cowboy Commandments" some thirty years later, stipulates that a cowboy must be fair, truthful, tolerant, hard-working, "gentle with children, elderly people and animals," and (here twentieth-century morality weighs in) a respecter of "women, parents and his nation's laws," a non-smoker and non-drinker, and a patriot.

In an evocative passage in *The Virginian* Wister contrasted the town of Medicine Bow, "this wretched husk of squalor," with what lay outside its "very doors," "a world of crystal light, a land without end, a space across which Noah and Adam might come straight from Genesis." Charlie Russell's take on Western space was slightly different. "Speakin' of liars," he wrote,

> the Old West could put in its claim for
> more of em than any other land under
> the sun. The mountains and plains
> seemed to stimulate man's imagination.
> A man in the States might have been a liar in a
> small way, but when he comes west he soon takes lessons from
> the prairies, where ranges a hundred miles away seem within touchin'
> distance, streams run uphill and Nature appears to lie some herself.

ABOVE
Program for "The Virginian"
Printed paper, 1909

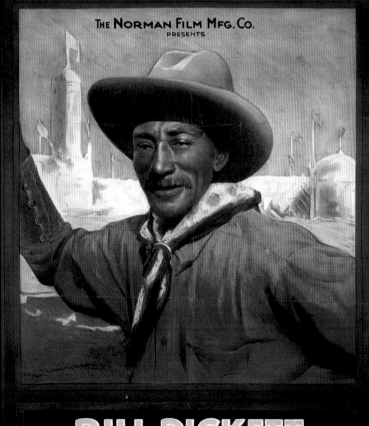

ABOVE
Advertisement for "A. Bauer"
Features C. M. Russell
"poker game" image.
Clinton and Co., Chicago, Illinois
Lithograph on paper

LEFT
Movie Poster for The Bulldogger
Norman Film Mfg. Company,
Jacksonville, Florida
Ritchey Litho. Corporation, 1922
Lithograph on paper

RIGHT
Advertising Tray for "Heptol Splits"
Chicago, Illinois, ca. 1904
After a 1904 painting by C.M. Russell.
Lithograph on tin

After a decade on the range whooping it up with the other young cowpunchers, Russell turned to painting full-time in 1893, married in 1896, and settled down to earn his reputation as the Cowboy Artist. Like Remington, he created his own iconic Western imagery. A tray advertising Heptol Splits, "The Perfect Laxative," featured a 1904 Russell painting of a bucking horse and rider (the appropriateness of the imagery requires no comment), while an earlier chromolithographic advertisement for C.A. Bauer, a Chicago liquor distributor, used a Russell grouping of an Indian, a Chinese and a cowboy playing poker. The point of the advertisement is obscure, since Bauer issued a pair of prints, a before and after scene, that removed fair play from the cowboy code in favor of the persuasion of a drawn revolver. Perhaps the cowboy is supposed to be Sam. Toughnut, the name nailed above one of the cabin doors, while the Chinese is presumably the laundryman Hop Lee. It is a bit of antiquated humor, unsavory to current sensibilities perhaps, but it does conjure up the Wild West, and a rougher side to the cowboy's appeal.[40]

Indeed, though ethnic variety was a fact of Western life, apart from Indians it had little impact on popular imagery. Black cowboys were common, especially in the Southwest; but a poster showing a black cowboy, such as rodeo star Bill Pickett, is rare. The Wild West shows all featured women, not just as trick riders and deadeye rifle shots in the Annie Oakley mode, but, in the early years of rodeo, as full-fledged bronc riders. Russell tipped his hat to them in 1925. "The girl bronk rider is new for me," he wrote in forwarding a sketch of one, "and if Harison Fisher [Charles Dana] Gibson or aney of those Girl painters would see it they might get sore and say I was crouding thair range but I saw a Gibson Cow boy and Il admit my Cow Girl dont look near as lady like as his Cow puncher did." Today cowgirls have been rediscovered and are very much in vogue, but the amount of cowgirl memorabilia around establishes an older pedigree.[41]

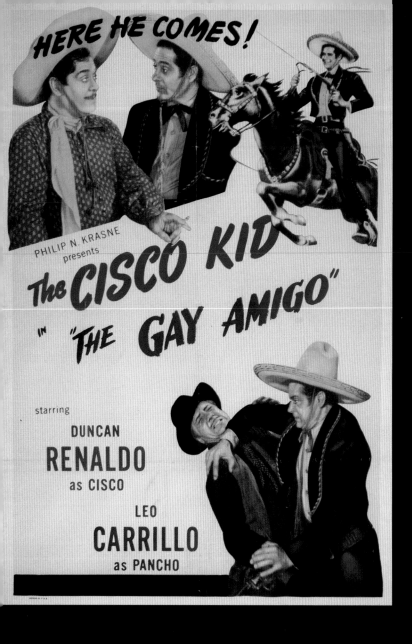

Annie Oakley Cased Pistols, Shotgun and Target Balls
L.C. Smith Shotgun: Serial # 44937, 12 Gauge, trap grade, 1899
Portrait of Oakley appears on lockplates; her signature is gold inlaid on triggerguard.
Hunter Arms Company with engraving by Tiffany and Company, New York

Cased ensemble of pistols assembled as a gift for Annie Oakley from her husband Frank Butler.
Stevens-Gould Model No.37, Single-shot pistol: Serial # 10591, .22 caliber, ca. 1890
Smith and Wesson First Model, Single-shot pistol: Serial # 105090, .22 caliber, 1890
Smith and Wesson Model No.3 Revolver: Serial # 27941, .44 caliber, 1892

Glass Target Ball: Faceted amber color, Bogardus patent, 1877

Glass Target Ball: Smooth amber color, Paine patent, 1877
Target balls donated by Alex Kerr

OPPOSITE PAGE
Book "The Covered Wagon"
Emerson Hough with dust jacket art by W.H.D. Koerner
D. Appleton and Co., 1922

ABOVE
Beaded Buckskin Jacket
Buckskin with beadwork, ribbons and silver buttons, ca. 1913.
Worn by rodeo rider Odille O. Jones in the Miller
Brothers 101 Ranch Wild West Show, this outfit was
made by another cowgirl who also rode for the Miller
Brothers. Odille loved to ride into the arena with the
feel of the beaded fringe tapping her on the back as
it moved in the breeze.

The Western hero is a type—a white male with a certain set of values. In the pantheon of popular screen heroes, Cisco Kid was the notable exception, evolving through various personifications into a Don Quixote, a man of generosity and honor in a knockout Mexican costume. Ordinarily ethnics have played the role of Cisco's sidekick Pancho, as supporting characters and faithful companions. The pairing of a Lone Ranger and Tonto or a Red Ryder and Little Beaver fits within a cultural tradition reaching back to Robinson Crusoe and his Man Friday, a Caribbean native whose unflinching loyalty to his white superior is his distinguishing characteristic. The fifth of Gene Autry's Cowboy Commandments preached racial and religious tolerance. But this ideal fit within the broader spectrum of the hero's duty towards those weaker than himself and dependent on him for protection—women, children, the elderly, animals, other races. One of the requirements for a William S. Hart movie was that he have "opportunities to come to the screen rescue of suffering and imperilled femininity." It is the condescending assumptions built into the hero's relations with those he champions that have led to the proliferation of

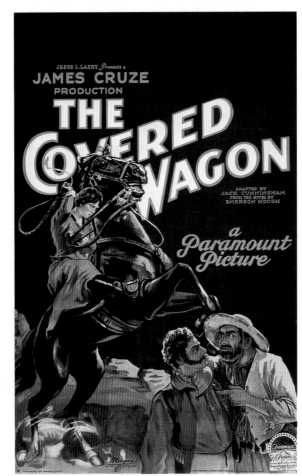

payback Westerns like *Posse* (1993), *Bad Girls* (1994) and *The Quick and the Dead* (1995), where blacks and women take matters into their own hands. The point of the cult of the cowgirl is that she requires no rescuing by William S. Hart, but he might require rescuing from her. A fact worthy of note is that the strong-woman tradition, like that of the cowgirl, has long roots. The dust jacket for Emerson Hough's 1922 novel *The Covered Wagon* might show the pioneer woman as a prairie madonna, but the poster for the movie the next year transformed her into a bullwhip artist.

In 1954 as the *Cattle Queen of Montana*, Barbara Stanwyck stripped off her petticoats and strapped on her guns. But it has been since *Thelma*

Right
Movie Poster for The Covered Wagon
Morgan Litho Co., Cleveland, Ohio, 1923
Lithograph on paper

& *Louise* (1991) that virtually all revisionist Westerns have favored culturally-sensitive men and ballsy women on a tear—Western heroes for our age.[42]

In the late nineteenth century, the Western myth expressed anxieties harbored by an Anglo-Saxon elite. The myth took a peculiar form, a repudiation of things Eastern by Easterners who praised the West as a healthy alternative to an increasingly sickly East. This requires explanation. The suspicion that the East—which in reality dominated the West culturally, politically and economically—had become a sickly appendage to the body politic was fostered by mostly privileged Eastern men who lamented the waning of those rough-hewn pioneering traits that, they believed, had made the nation great. Wealth was to blame, certainly, for having produced a pampered class long on its comforts and short on moral fiber. And immigration was a major problem. Since the Civil War the scourings of Europe had inundated America, accounting for labor unrest in the cities and everything else unpleasant. There was something rotten in the land. But out West, ah, there men were still men, the old values pertained, and life-affirming challenges abounded. Out there was the real America. Roosevelt believed this, and Remington and Wister, and they used their talents to persuade others.[43]

The initiation of the tenderfoot was a favorite theme in Western lore. Remington illustrated it for an essay by Roosevelt published in *Century Magazine* in 1888. He showed a sneering cowboy firing his revolver at the feet of an effete Easterner—"Dance Higher—Dance Faster," it was titled. Cowboys, Roosevelt explained, "shoot off boot-heels or tall hats occasionally, or make some obnoxious butt 'dance' by shooting round his feet; but they rarely meddle in this way with men who have not themselves played the fool." Wister, foremost among dudes, had his narrator/alter ego plaintively comment in *The Virginian* that in the West "thieves are presumed innocent until proved guilty, but a starched collar is condemned at once." It was all in good fun, of course, a rite of passage. The dude who showed grit easily won over his Western tormentors and, according to popular tradition, ended up in the bar buying a round to toast his newfound acceptance. The image of the crow-hopping dude functioned like a Puritan jeremiad: it rehearsed the punishment for past transgressions while holding out hope for redemption. Repent the error of your ways, or suffer the consequences. Teddy Roosevelt was a model of successful transformation. It did not hurt that he owned the ranch in Dakota Territory where he lived from 1883 to 1886. But the key to his success out West was fitting in with the boys and proving his mettle. In March 1886 he led two of his cowboys in pursuit of three thieves who stole a boat from his Elkhorn Ranch and made off with it down the Missouri. Cold weather would not stand between Roosevelt and justice. After a three-day chase, the boat and the campfire of the thieves hove into view. "For a moment we felt a thrill

LEFT
Movie Poster for Cattle Queen of Montana
RKO Pictures, 1954
Lithograph on paper

BELOW
Melodrama Poster for The Cow-Boy Girl
ca. 1900
Ackerman-Quigley, New York
Lithograph on paper

of keen excitement, and our veins tingled as we crept cautiously towards the fire, for it seemed likely there would be a brush," Roosevelt recalled, "but, as it turned out, this was almost the only moment of much interest, for the capture itself was as tame as possible." Nevertheless, his Colt revolver and the Winchester he carried on the pursuit of the thieves became treasured mementos of a Western experience that helped define his public image as the Roughrider president.[44]

Roosevelt's mention of the "butt" being made to dance to the tune of a six-shooter occurred in an essay he titled "Frontier Types." In contrast to the hapless dude were "the old race of Rocky Mountain hunters and trappers." Clad in buckskin, "the most picturesque and distinctively national dress ever worn in America," they steered the way West "across the flat and endless seas of grass," and in the process honed their character. "Frank, bold, and self-reliant to a degree," fearing "neither man, brute, nor element," loyal to their friends and vindictive to their enemies, they were, in sum, "the arch-type of freedom." Next came the cowboy with his "fine, manly qualities": "Brave, hospitable, hardy, and adventurous, he is the grim pioneer of our race; he prepares the way for the civilization from before whose face he must himself disappear." In a few paragraphs, Roosevelt had summed up the qualities of Western myth, from space and its shaping influence on character through to the transience that made it poignant. The Western hero was simply a refined version of the frontier type.[45]

AN ART AND ITS THEMES

Typing was the essence of genre painting, which flourished in America in the three decades before the Civil War. Scenes of ordinary people and everyday life were all the vogue, consistent with Walt Whitman's celebration in *Leaves of Grass* (1855) of "the word Democratic, the word En-Masse." In ordinariness was the strength of America, the key to the political experiment that was the envy of the world. It was also the basis of a distinctive national art. Typical farmers, Yankees, Southerners, frontiersmen, blacks, women, urban urchins and working men peopled this art as, it was thought, they peopled America. "As fictions that they created about one another, types and typical behavior gave pundits, storytellers, editorialists, and audiences across the regions quick points of reference," Elizabeth Johns has written. But typing by its very nature substitutes the appearance of reality for reality which, messy as ever, defies neat categorization. This limitation, made starkly evident by the Civil War, helped ring the curtain down on what had come to seem a hopelessly sentimental tradition. There was, Johns observes, one exception. Types continued to flourish in what has been called "exotic genre," or Western art:

OPPOSITE PAGE
Revolver, holster and rifle belonging to Theodore Roosevelt with book he wrote.
Colt Single Action Revolver: .44-40 caliber, Hartford, Connecticut, 1883, engraving by L.D. Nimschke of New York, carried by Roosevelt during his years in Dakota Territory.
Revolver Holster: J.S. Collins and Company, Cheyenne, Wyoming, ca. 1885. Tooled leather
Winchester Lever Action Carbine: Model 1876, .40 caliber, New Haven, Connecticut, 1886, engraved by L.D. Nimschke, New York. Used to hunt deer and antelope. Was carried by Roosevelt in the capture of boat thieves.
Ranch Life and the Hunting Trail, by Theodore Roosevelt. New York: The Century Company, 1888.
Acquisition of these items was made possible in part by Paul S. And June A. Ebensteiner.

The one continuation from the early genre painting to the imagery of late in the century was the type of the Western trapper or hunter. First developed by [Charles] Deas and [William T.] Ranney, and then simplified by [Arthur Fitzwilliam] Tait for mass production, the figure became a prototype for the revered cowboys of Frederic Remington and Charles Russell, and later for the Western male adventurer in twentieth-century films, videos, and advertising.

Like typing itself, this is too simplistic. The importance accorded Remington within the Western art tradition is undeniable, but his fondness for types came out of the imperatives of illustration, where effective generalization was the order of the day and types abounded long after the vogue of genre painting had passed.[46]

What the Western illustrator did was arrange types within various settings. Remington in his illustrations frequently ignored landscape, allowing his actors to perform their roles on a table-flat surface that evoked the Western space of plains and desert. His visual shorthand equates with the dime novelist's narrative technique. "Aesthetically, the unlimited openness of the western landscape is perhaps the most functional aspect of the Western's setting, for open space offers the reader a bird's eye view of the action continually unfolding—often simultaneously—on various parts of the landscape," Daryl Jones has written. "It is helpful to think of the dime novel Western's standardized setting as a vast gameboard upon which opposing pieces are carefully moved to or from distinct,

prearranged areas." Generic types, interchangeable settings, typical action: Frederic Remington's West. Art worked, through repetition of select themes, to reinforce the narrative structure of Western myth.[47]

Following two excursions up the Missouri River in the late 1850s, the St. Louis painter Carl Wimar abandoned the set history pieces that were his specialty during four years of study in Germany. Clash and conflict dominated these imaginary contrivances showing the woodsy world of Daniel

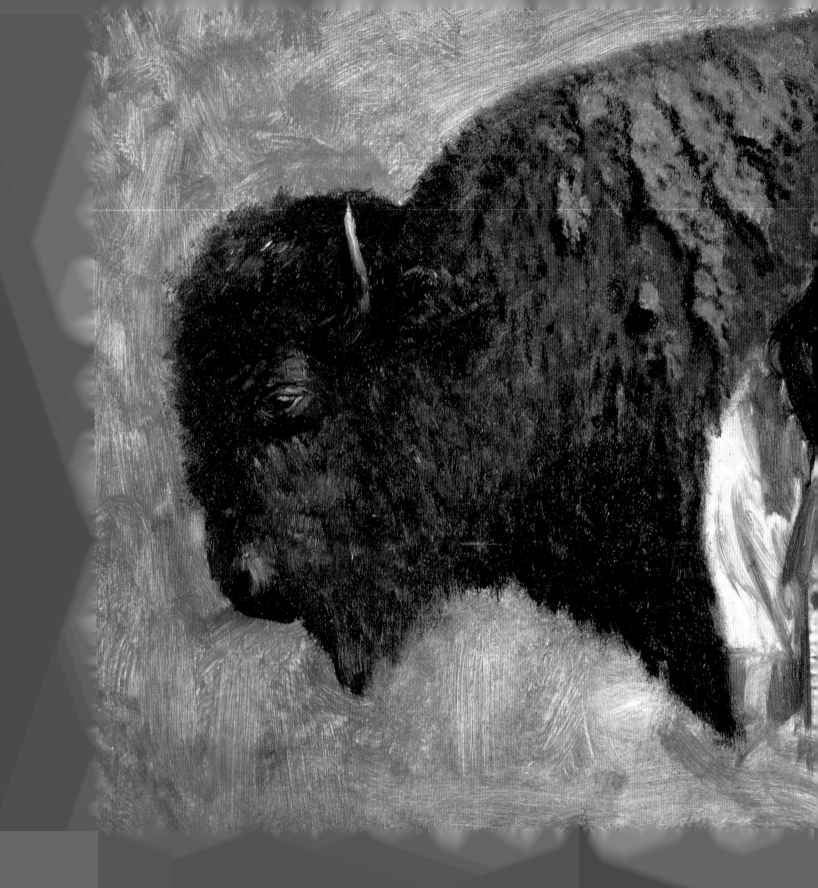

Boone, golden-tressed maidens being borne off to captivity, and skulking warriors rising from the tall prairie grass to swoop down on emigrant trains, steal horses and flee from pursuing dragoons. Seeing the Far West firsthand transformed Wimar's vision. An expansive theater opened before him; Western light flooded his eyes, and his themes changed. Instead of border conflict, he painted great herds of buffalo and Indian peoples inhabiting a vast land awash in the sunset colors that foretold their mutual fate. In grand vistas, glowing ribbons of river snaked their way through stands of trees and around distant bluffs, carrying the eye westward to where the horizon bled into the flaming sky. Charlie Russell loved Wimar's glowing romanticism. His paintings are serene and urgent. They show beginnings and endings. You must see this West, they say, before it passes, and time closes in on spacious dreaming.[48]

ANTICIPATION

There is in Western art a quality of hushed expectancy: the natural world awaiting something to impinge upon it. The landscape, certainly, before the trees were turned into lumber, the water harnessed for power or irrigation, the mountains mined, the grasslands plowed. And the native peoples. Commencing in the 1830s, several artists—Karl Bodmer, Alfred Jacob Miller, Seth Eastman, John Mix Stanley, Charles Deas, Paul Kane—visited the Western tribes or resided among them in an official capacity. Every one of them was more or less influenced by George Catlin, who made four trips West in the years 1832-36 and formed an Indian Gallery of more than 300 portraits and 200 paintings showing everyday activities. Embracing some fifty North American tribes, the Gallery constituted a documentary record of Indian life infused with emotion and charged with meaning, because Catlin was persuaded that the Indians he had visited, inhabiting a "fairy-land" and blissfully unaware of the forces bearing down upon them, were on the brink of catastrophic change.[49]

In 1847 Charles Deas painted *Indian Warrior on the Edge of a Precipice*. It bears comparison to Eastman's *Indian on the Lookout* and Stanley's *Young Chief Uncas* from the same period. In each, a lone Indian, seated on a promontory and armed with a tomahawk, stares into space. Deas' Indian dangles one foot over a rushing waterfall that feeds the lake behind. Soaring eagles and a nest in a tree below suggest the great height he occupies. He is literally on the brink, yet unconcerned. It is up to the viewer to provide the sequel. This hardy warrior, muscular and confident, is doomed. The land he guards is destined to belong to the enterprising pioneers of another culture. The cause is already lost, but he does not know it. He is the lookout for a vanishing race.[50]

Deas lived in St. Louis, where Charlie Russell grew up. About 1890, a decade after he had moved to Montana, Russell painted a seated Indian of his own, *Indian Girl*. She perches on the edge of a cliff, chin cupped in hand, a sunset sky behind. The painting expresses romantic yearning, and a prophecy fulfilled. In the less than half century since Deas completed *Indian Warrior on the Edge of a Precipice*, a series of battles had been fought in the West, terminating with the slaughter of the Lakota at Wounded Knee in late December 1890. Indian resistance was a thing of the past, and Western tribes, under the General Allotment Act of 1887, faced the final breakup of the reservation remnants of Indian Country. According to the allotment policy's chief architect, it was "the beginning of the end of the Indian as an Indian." Native cultures, at least, were slated to vanish through a policy of total assimilation

that, like allotment in severalty, would prove (quoting from Theodore Roosevelt's First Annual Message to Congress) "a mighty pulverizing engine to break up the tribal mass." John Hauser's turn-of-the-century portrait *Wild Horse* provides a visual equivalent. It shows a standing figure in red blanket, fur cap, and beaded moccasins, holding a rifle—the Indian as an Indian within the understood conventions. But at his feet is a buffalo skull, artistic shorthand for the end of his traditional way of life. Indian and buffalo had long served as symbols for the passing West, making the buffalo skull an especially potent juxtaposition. Like the buffalo/Indian head nickel first coined in 1913, Wild Horse stood for yesterday. The Old West was gone, and with it America's youth.[51]

WILD HORSE WINNEBAGO RES.   John Hauser 1902

Instead of pathos, a sense of wonder informs paintings depicting the vanguard of white settlement arriving on the Western scene. They are embarking on the future, the world all before them. Since the Lewis and Clark Expedition was the first formal exploration of America's Far West, it is fitting that Thomas M. Burnham celebrate the spirit of discovery in *The Lewis and Clark Expedition* (ca. 1850) by isolating the two commanders at the moment they top a rise. Their men trail behind, where we see a forest whose floor is brushed by the light from a lemony sky; ahead, another forest, massive and dark, awaits them. One of the captains gestures towards the trees in front—the yet unknown. If discovery entails a degree of tension, William T. Ranney's *The Trappers* (1856) is about pure joy. Two mountain men in buckskins ride side by side, chatting and at ease. A soft glow illuminates the banks and the stream in which they ride, turning it into a highway of light. It is beaver-rich, judging from the gnawed branches in the foreground. Nature's bounty overflows. "For a transitory enchanted moment," man has indeed found "something commensurate to his capacity for wonder."

In an influential study of Western film, Jim Kitses observed: "What gives the form a particular thrust and centrality is . . . its being placed at exactly that moment when options are still open, the dream of primitivistic individualism, the ambivalence of at once beneficent and threatening horizons, still tenable." In the end, the Western myth offers no reprieve for white or red. Eventually, Ranney's trappers will run out of room. Their idyll will be shattered, limits imposed, and options closed. But that mythic moment is the point: men in open space, forever verging on something unrealizable. Phantoms, after all, can only be pursued, not captured. There is a fugitive quality to the West: even at its most tranquil, it is a world on the run.[52]

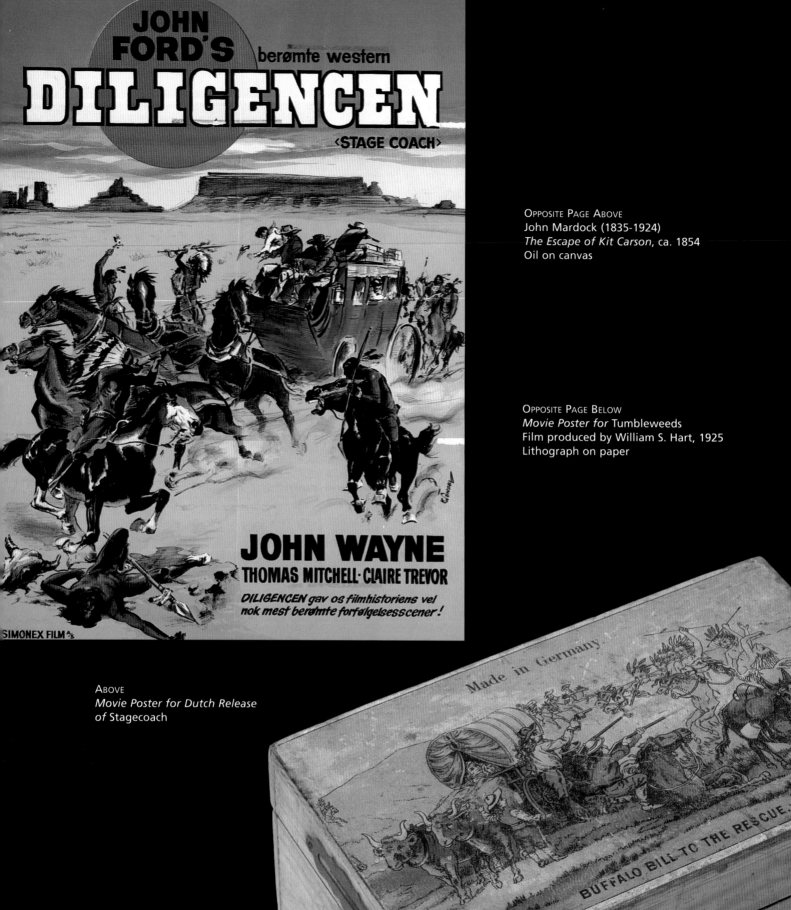

JOHN FORD'S berømte western

DILIGENCEN

⟨STAGE COACH⟩

JOHN WAYNE

THOMAS MITCHELL · CLAIRE TREVOR

DILIGENCEN gav os filmhistoriens vel nok mest berømte forfølgelsesscener!

SIMONEX FILM A/s

OPPOSITE PAGE ABOVE
John Mardock (1835-1924)
The Escape of Kit Carson, ca. 1854
Oil on canvas

OPPOSITE PAGE BELOW
Movie Poster for Tumbleweeds
Film produced by William S. Hart, 1925
Lithograph on paper

ABOVE
Movie Poster for Dutch Release of Stagecoach

RIGHT
Toy Bank "Buffalo Bill to the Rescue"
Germany, ca. 1910
Lithographed paper and wood

Made in Germany

BUFFALO BILL TO THE RESCUE,

FLIGHT

The horseback chase is such a classic element of Western movies that it should have been a cinematic invention. It answered all the needs of motion picture storytelling in the era of silent film: life-and-death action, horses at full gallop, guns blazing, dust rising. In his spoken prologue to the 1939 re-release of his 1925 epic *Tumbleweeds,* William S. Hart recalled the thrill of making Westerns:

> The rush of the wind that cuts your face, the pounding hoofs of the pursuing posse, out there in front a fallen tree trunk that spans a yawning chasm, with a noble animal under you that takes it in the same low, ground-eating gallop. The harmless shots of the baffled ones that remain behind . . . and then, the clouds of dust . . .

In 1952 Gene Autry explained the formula for a successful television Western: "Keep it simple, keep it moving, keep it close and make it fast." Formulas require repetition. The chase is an essential Western cliche.[53]

But the chase was also perfect for arena entertainment, and years before the invention of moving pictures, Buffalo Bill's Wild West standardized a routine in which a Deadwood stagecoach circled the ring pursued by a howling war party, with Buffalo Bill riding to the rescue. This was such a popular feature of the Wild West—flight and double pursuit—that it entered vernacular culture in the charming form of a toy bank manufactured in Germany around 1910 showing "Buffalo Bill to the Rescue." But even Buffalo Bill did not begin it all. The chase was established in Western iconography by the middle of the nineteenth century when William Ranney painted an action picture that he called *The Retreat* (1850) showing three trappers racing for their lives from pursuing Indians. Two years later Arthur Fitzwilliam Tait paid it homage in *The Prairie Hunter, "One Rubbed Out."* A lone trapper turns in his saddle to admire the effects of a well-placed shot at four Indian pursuers. His horse, wild-eyed and at full gallop, is straining to escape; the trapper, in contrast, exhibits a professional calm. He is the self-reliant Western hero riding through an open country that can offer no protection or escape. Everything rests on his demonstrated competence. Since he occupies the foreground, he seems more than a match for the trailing party of Indians already reduced by one-quarter. Almost all paintings of flight and pursuit adopted the same compositional strategy: a rider dashing pellmell towards the viewer, commanding sympathy in his race for life. He symbolizes the sacrifices of pioneering in a visual form laden with visceral appeal.

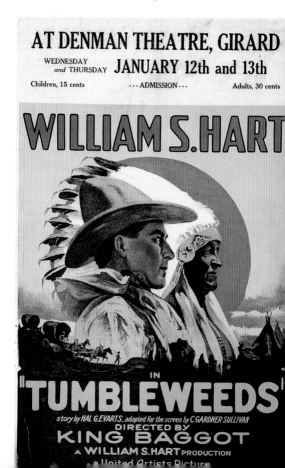

AT DENMAN THEATRE, GIRARD

WEDNESDAY and THURSDAY JANUARY 12th and 13th

Children, 15 cents --- ADMISSION --- Adults, 30 cents

WILLIAM S. HART

IN

"TUMBLEWEEDS"

story by HAL G. EVARTS, adapted for the screen by C. GARDNER SULLIVAN

DIRECTED BY KING BAGGOT

A WILLIAM S. HART PRODUCTION

Flight is a theme with universal implications. Ranney saw the West in the mid-1830s when he joined in the struggle for Texas independence; Tait, an Englishman who arrived in New York in 1850, never did. But he was influenced by Ranney's work, and borrowed costume bits from him to provide authentic details in the thirteen different Western scenes he painted between 1851 and 1862. Eight, including *The Prairie Hunter*, were issued as prints by what became the firm of Currier & Ives. Consequently, Tait had an influence in defining Western imagery out of all proportion to his meager output, and his meager knowledge. But authenticity was irrelevant anyway, the details merely serving to corroborate entirely imaginary constructs. Imagination was the artist's real power. Frederick Faust, who under the pen name Max Brand was the most prolific creator of formula Westerns in the twentieth century, had one basic rule: do not go West. Live in Italy, like he did much of the time. The West was a myth. Going West could contribute nothing to the formula, and might even spoil it all. Frederic Remington, renowned as a Western realist, made that very point in 1900 when he wrote to his wife from Santa Fe, "Shall never come west again—It is all brick buildings—derby hats and blue overhauls—it spoils my early illusions—and they are my capital."[54]

Illusions were Remington's stock in trade. He knew this, and if his realistic mode confused his viewers into not knowing, well, that was the intention. Western art tapped into the desire to escape from mundane reality; it posited its own reality. For Remington, flight was an essential theme. His 1901 equestrian bronze *The Cheyenne* frees the figure from narrative itself. Harry Jackson's *Pony Express* tells a story as the rider looks back and fires at unseen pursuers; Remington's Cheyenne warrior is simply racing by, whether the pursuer or the pursued unknown. He could be a figure from *Blood Meridian*, where the distinction disappears, and the only moral imperative is to ride on.

RIGHT
Harry Jackson
Pony Express 1967
Bronze, polychrome, casting number 12 of 20,
Donated by Dr. and Mrs. M. William Lockard

RIGHT
Frederic Reminington (1861-1909)
The Cheyenne, 1901
Bronze, casting number 65
Roman Bronze Works, New York
Donated by Mr. and Mrs. Gene Autry

ABOVE
Arthur Fitzwilliam Tait (1819-1909)
The Prairie hunter, "One Rubbed Out"
Oil on canvas, 1852

ABOVE
Alexander Edouart (1818-1892)
The Chase, 1857-58
Oil on canvas
This painting depicts Henry L. Ford, a captain in General
John C. Fremont's California Battalion, being chased by
Californio lancers in California during the U.S.-Mexican
War. Ford took part in the 1846 Bear Flag Revolt at
Sonoma and in 1857 commissioned San Francisco artist
Alexander Edouart to paint several scenes recalling
his adventures.

OPPOSITE PAGE ABOVE
Frederic Remington (1861-1909)
Leaving the Canyon, ca. 1889
Published in *The Cosmopolitan*, October, 1894.
Wash and ink on paper

BELOW
Frederic Remington (1861-1909)
An Episode in the Opening Up of Cattle Country, 1887
Published in *Century Illustrated Magazine*, 1888 and in
Ranch Life and the Hunting Trail by Theodore Roosevelt, 1888
Oil on board

STAND AND DELIVER

The chase was prelude to the desperate stand, a Remington favorite showing a party of trappers or cowboys or soldiers forced to dismount and confront their destiny. Flight was over, the end at hand. Such was the cost of civilized progress, Remington always implied, though he knew perfectly well that few Custer's Last Stands ever followed, and overwhelmingly it was the Indians at bay, not the vanguards of white civilization. Nevertheless, in his younger days he cheered on the winning of the West without a thought for the losers. For him, as for the champions of Manifest Destiny half a century earlier, Anglo-Saxon supremacy in America was foreordained

and right. There is an inescapable irony in a painting like Alexander Edouart's *The War in California*. Done about ten years after the fact, in 1857-58, it shows an American officer being pursued by *Californio* lancers. They are defending their country; he is the invader. But like the Indians chasing trappers and cowboys over the deserts and plains of Western art, the Mexicans have become the aggressors. They will be the losers in the end, their land the forfeit. But within the logic of the chase, the American officer is both the victim and the hero. Consider two swords, one presented to Major Edgar S. Hawkins, 7th U.S. Infantry, on August 13 1846; the other taken from the body of Lieutenant Colonel Juan N. Najera a month later. Hawkins' sword, inscribed in honor of the successful defense of Fort Brown on the Rio Grande during a siege by Mexican soldiers,

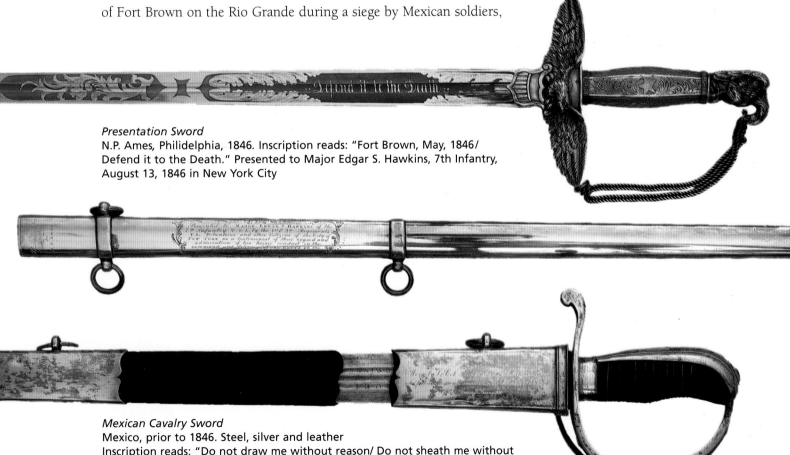

Presentation Sword
N.P. Ames, Philidelphia, 1846. Inscription reads: "Fort Brown, May, 1846/
Defend it to the Death." Presented to Major Edgar S. Hawkins, 7th Infantry,
August 13, 1846 in New York City

Mexican Cavalry Sword
Mexico, prior to 1846. Steel, silver and leather
Inscription reads: "Do not draw me without reason/ Do not sheath me without
honor." Owned by Lieutenant Colonel Juan Najera
Donated by Mrs. Grace W. Hays

reads, "Defend it to the Death"; Najera's sword, carried by him during the unsuccessful defense of Monterrey, is inscribed, "Draw me not without cause/Sheathe me not without honor." Winners and losers. George Armstrong Custer owned a sword inscribed with the same chivalric sentiment. Unlike Colonel Najera, however, he got to be one of history's winners by losing, and in the process winning mythic immortality as a martyr to the cause of pioneering.

An illustration by Remington published in 1894 is suggestive for its treatment as much as for its subject matter. Titled *Leaving the Canyon*, it shows a white officer, posed hands on hips, watching African-

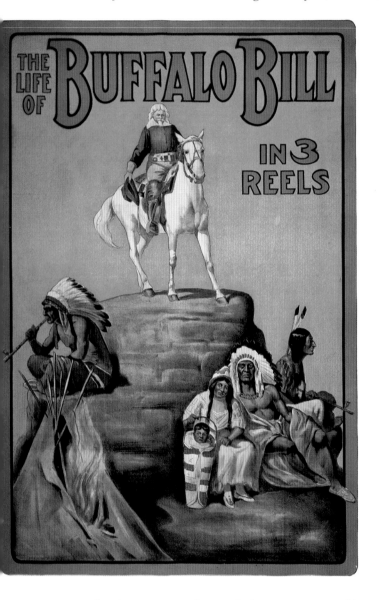

American troopers of the Tenth Cavalry transporting a wounded Apache up a steep incline. All are literally under his command. In composition and message Remington's illustration bears a striking resemblance to *The Life of Buffalo Bill in 3 Reels*, a poster issued by the Buffalo Bill-Pawnee Bill Film Company in 1910 showing the old scout astride his white horse atop a promontory with the Indians he has conquered and now befriended camped on the slopes below. In both, racial dominance is indicated by a pyramidical composition that draws the eye to the white man on top. Its didactic power is evident in any Custer's Last Stand, where the imagery overrides what happened (the Indians won) to assert a higher lesson, what Walt Whitman called "a trumpet note for heroes":
Continues yet the old, old legend of our race! The loftiest of life upheld by death! The ancient banner perfectly maintained! (O lesson opportune—O how I welcome thee!)
In Tompkins H. Matteson's *Custer's Last Stand* (1878) and the six-sheet poster

for the 1925 re-release of Thomas H. Ince's film *Custer's Last Fight*, the composition *is* the lesson, representing visually a cultural ideal. Like Christ at Calvary, Custer stands on a desolate Western hill, composed and unafraid, sacrificing self to cause, setting an example that will inspire reverence and awe. Last stands erase the actuality of Indian defeat and shift the moral burden of conquest by making the victors victims in an equal war.[55]

BATTLE OF THE LITTLE BIGHORN

FOREPAUGH'S EQUESTRIAN SPECTACULAR TRAGEDY

The years are but half a score,
And the war-whoop sounds no more
With the blast of bugles, where
Straight into a slaughter-pen,
With his doomed three hundred men,
Rode the chief with the yellow hair.
—Whittier.

DEATH OF CUSTER

AVIL PRINTING CO. PHILA.

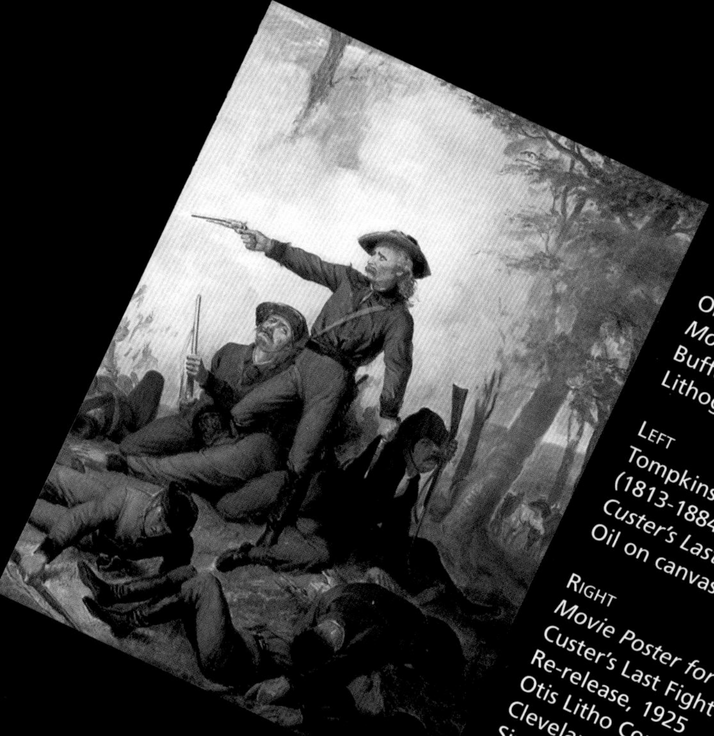

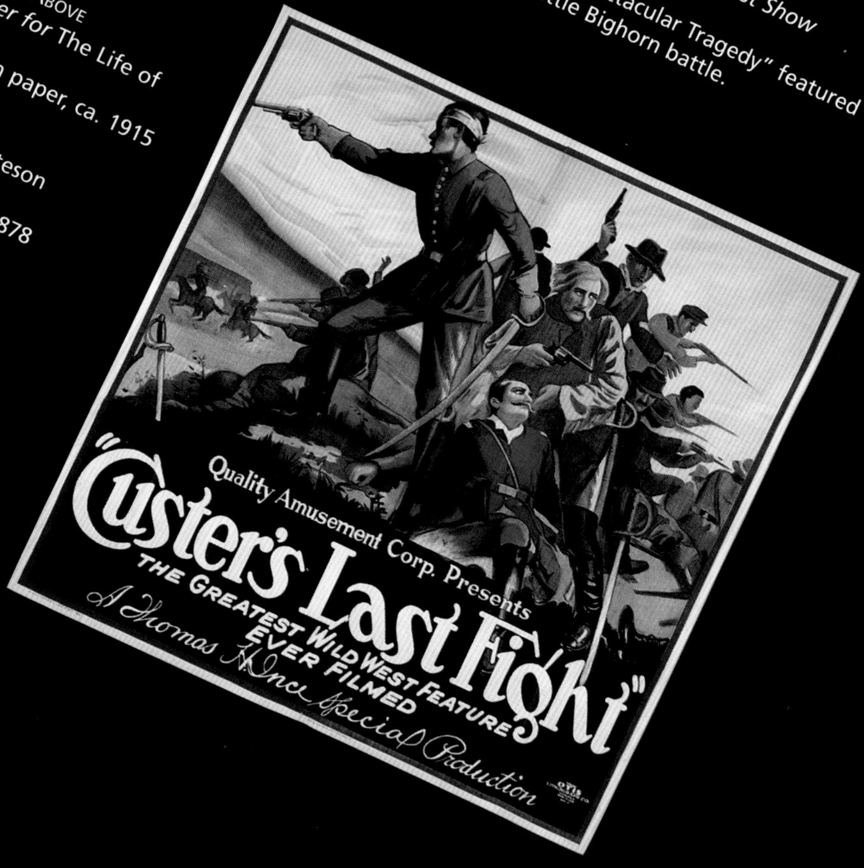

ABOVE
Advertising card for Forepaugh Wild West Show
Lithograph on card, ca 1890
"Forepaugh's Equestrian Spectacular Tragedy" featured
a reenactment of the Little Bighorn battle.

OPPOSITE PAGE ABOVE
Movie Poster for The Life of
Buffalo Bill
Lithograph on paper, ca. 1915

LEFT
Tompkins H. Matteson
(1813-1884)
Custer's Last Shot, 1878
Oil on canvas

RIGHT
Movie Poster for
Custer's Last Fight
Re-release, 1925
Otis Litho Company,
Cleveland, Ohio
Six-sheet lithograph on paper

Quality Amusement Corp. Presents
"Custer's Last Fight"
THE GREATEST WILD WEST FEATURE
EVER FILMED
A Thomas H. Ince Special Production

LEFT
Movie Poster for Redskin
Paramount Pictures, 1929
Lithograph on paper

RIGHT
Soup Spoon and Ice Cream Server
Sterling silver with gold gilt, 1890-1895
Designed by Charles Grosjean
Tiffany and Company, New York

OPPOSITE PAGE BELOW
Hair Comb
Maker unknown, ca. 1850
Tortoise shell

RIGHT
Upright Piano
Manufactured by Steinway and Sons,
New York, 1903
Painted panels by Edwin Willard Deming
(1860-1942)
Commissioned by the Doheny family of
Los Angeles, California

CLOSURE

Western art at the end of the nineteenth century rounded out the mythic narrative. From wilderness to anticipation and from flight to the determined stand, it carried the story through to closure.

Charles Russell preferred painting horizontal compositions. They allowed ample elbow room for his Western types to go about their business. But in the color prints that by 1905 were broadcasting his images everywhere, his composition was routinely tightened by deleting some of the landscape. Thus the borders closed in on Russell's spacious West. This seems an apt metaphor for all the changes he deplored. Barbed wire had fenced in the open range, confining space and curtailing freedom. In a letter to a Montana senator, the artist in 1902 linked the fate of the Indian to that of the Old West generally. "Speaking of gamblers," he wrote,

reminds me several years ago when games were wide open I sat at a faryo layout in Chinook the hour was lat and the play light a good deal of talk passed over the green bord the subject of conversation was the Indian question the dealor Kicking George was an old time sport who spoke of cards as an industry . . . the Kicker alloud an Injun had no more right in this country than a Cyote I told him what he said might be right but there were folks coming to the country on the new rail road that thaught the same way about gamblers an he wouldent winter maney times till hed find out the wild Indian would go but would onley brake the trail for the gambler. My prophecy came true we still have the gambler but like the cyote civilization has made him an outlaw

"Trails plowed under" became Russell's personal epitaph for the Old West, summing up his recognition of closure.[56]

The fate of that Indian warrior perched on edge of a precipice in Charles Deas' painting had passed from prophecy to fact. Assimilation was working; the old-time Indian was over the brink. The distinctive cultures Catlin had portrayed were blending into the American mainstream. Proof positive was a turn-of-the-century vogue for decorative mementos of the old-time Indian. The public might have to settle for befeathered warriors on pennies and stamps and trading cards; the wealthy could afford a little more—perhaps a silver service by Tiffany's featuring dancing Indians based on Catlin prototypes, or a Steinway piano decorated with Indian scenes by Edwin W. Deming, who painted the red men's soul, taking "no cognizance or their existence as a modern disorganized race." This was nothing new, really. The Vanishing Indian had

inspired regret throughout the nineteenth century, and American culture had honored a romantic stereotype of the noble savage, the First American, in literary works, sentimental poetry, sculpture, coinage, and the decorative arts, even as real Indians were being displaced. The difference after 1890 was one of degree. The sculptor who later designed the buffalo/ Indian head nickel, James Earl Fraser, had given concrete form to the concept of the Vanishing Indian in a heroic-sized sculpture originally modelled in the 1890s. *The End of the Trail* showed an Indian man slumped on his exhausted horse. Placed where Fraser wanted it, on a cliff above the Pacific Ocean, it rendered the symbolic literal. The Indian as an Indian was finished. Let us kill the Indian, the founder of Carlisle Indian School said, "and save the man."[57]

In several of Frederic Remington's latelife paintings there was a similar exhaustion of hope. War in Cuba in 1898 had provided him a chance to see what he had long hankered after, men in real combat. He returned home chastened and saddened and resolved to stick to Western subjects. As his youthful exuberance faded, his vision darkened. *Only Alkali Water* (*The Waterhole*), done about 1906, is a case in point. It shows a mounted cowboy caked in dust wandering the bottom of a dry water hole, with nothing to slake the thirst of man or animal or stave off certain death. It was as though Remington had shifted his allegiance from winners to losers. A few years earlier he had painted a related work, *Fight for the Waterhole* (1903). A classic Remington desperate stand, it shows cowboys defending their position against circling Indians. The life-sustaining pool of water in the middle of the depression portends success. *The Waterhole*, in contrast, is a hollow cosmic joke, echoing a bleak poem from Stephen Crane's 1899 collection *War Is Kind*:

A man said to the universe:

"*Sir, I exist!*"

"*However,*" *replied the universe,*

"*The fact has not created in me*

A sense of obligation."

Horse and rider, rendered in dusty browns and greys, have reached the end of their trail. The fight is over without a shot being fired. The next year Remington told a reporter, "I have no interest whatever in the industrial West of to-day . . . My West passed utterly out of existence so long ago as to make it merely a dream. It put on its hat, took up its blankets and marched off the board; the curtain came down and a new act was in progress." Be grateful, the journalist concluded, "that in ringing down the final curtain on the great Wild-West drama the relentless course of empire has left to us at least one auditor with skill and enthusiasm and courage enough to perpetuate on canvas and in enduring bronze the most inspiriting phases of its colorful existence." Trails plowed under: the end of the trail. Westering, like Fraser's despondent Indian, was finished.[58]

TIMEBOUND: HISTORY'S IMPERATIVE

One of the drawings in Charlie Russell's boyhood sketchbook showed a buffalo herd drifting along the transcontinental railroad line, one magnificent bull pausing to rub against a telegraph pole. Whether Russell knew it or not, he had created an allegory for civilization's advance in the West. The

train bearing down in the distance symbolizes technological progress, while the buffalo stands for the old natural order that must soon yield way. Artists had worked many variations on this basic theme. Andrew Melrose's *Westward the Star of Empire Takes Its Way—Near Council Bluffs, Iowa* (1867) shows the train as an aggressive force, its blazing eye scattering nature before it. And where are the scrambling deer to go?—the forest has been leveled. What the train cannot do to subdue the wilderness, the settler's axe already has. John Gast's *American Progress* (1872) is even more explicitly allegorical. It shows the light of civilization dawning in the East, dispelling the darkness that enshrouds the West. Indians and buffalo retreat before the radiant figure of Progress, who floats through the air in a diaphanous gown, stringing telegraph wire with one hand, holding a school book in the other. Miners and farmers, a covered wagon, a Pony Express rider and a racing stagecoach keep pace, while three railroad trains nip at her heels. The buffalo bones on the plains below offer mute testimony to the price Progress demands.[59]

Railroad and telegraph lines stretching from coast to coast were the enemies of Western myth. They shut down the fantasy of endless space and opportunity even as they opened the way to more rapid development. Walt Whitman, who sang hosannas to that "resistless restless race" of American pioneers, celebrated the completion of the Pacific Railroad as the last link in a global communications network:

> *Passage to India!*
>
> *Lo, soul, seest thou not God's purpose from the first?*
>
> *The earth to be spann'd, connected by network,*
>
> *The races, neighbors, to marry and be given in marriage,*
>
> *The oceans to be cross'd, the distant brought near,*
>
> *The lands to be welded together.*

The dream that Columbus nurtured had been fulfilled:

> *(Ah Genoese thy dream! thy dream!*
>
> *Centuries after thou art laid in thy grave,*
>
> *The shore thou foundest verifies thy dream.)*

Whitman's triumphant ode raises issues pertinent to the current understanding of Western history. What verified one dream was a death-blow to others.[60]

The old triumphalist narrative of Western history, as it is now routinely called, tells a mostly sunny story of pioneer progress in a bountiful land. There were tests and trials, of course—starvation and privation, thirst and disappointment, battles with the Indians and the desert heat. Sacrifices were made, a human toll extracted. But in the end, the indomitable pioneer spirit won out, the land was settled, the deserts made to bloom. And Westward the course of empire took its way, completing the global circle, as Whitman would have it, of European culture. All told, a Happy Trails history of the West. The publication in 1987 of Patricia N. Limerick's *The Legacy of Conquest* helped set a different agenda in which defeat, not victory, and failure, not success, loom largest. A redirection along neglected trails, to the stories of ethnic diversity, of women and children and families, of institutions instead of individuals, of the mundane and ordinary instead of the exotic and colorful. Of life as it was lived, instead of Western fantasies. Of countless small realities in place of one great mythic swagger. Of toil and disillusionment instead of buoyancy and exuberance. Of outside domination instead of independence and freedom. Of complex cultural meetings instead of frontier lines dividing civilization and savagery. Of trash along the trails instead of an epic movement into empty space. In short, a large dose of reality to cure West-Fever. Stripped of its happy ending, Richard White has observed, Western history would become more tragedy than comedy. Its art would consist of paintings like Charles C. Nahl's *The Dead Miner* (1867), where the price of gold lust is life itself, and John D. Howland's *A Western Jury* (1883), showing a herd of buffalo milling around the body of a dead Indian. Furniture fashioned from buffalo horns, and even a splendid set of carved buffalo chairs created for a Scottish nobleman who loved to recall his hunting adventures

ABOVE
John D. Howland
A Western Jury, 1883
Oil on canvas

BELOW
Johnathan Gast (active 1870s)
American Progress, 1872
Oil on canvas

ABOVE
Buffalo Chairs
British Isles, 1842
Mahogany with rosewood horns and hooves, glass eyes

OPPOSITE PAGE
Parlor Chair
Pasadena, California, ca. 1895
Steer horn

ABOVE
White Swan (Crow)
Battle of Little Bighorn, ca. 1890
Crayon, watercolor and pencil on muslin

OPPOSITE PAGE
Charles Christian Nahl (1818-1878)
The Dead Miner, 1867
Oil on canvas

BELOW
John Williamson
Overland Route to Rocky Mountains, 1880
Oil on canvas

in the American West, would constitute an environmentalist reprimand. Our sympathies would be with the dispossessed Indians on the hill watching the wagon train pass by in John Williamson's *Overland Route to Rocky Mountains* (1880), instead of with the pioneers. Colonel Najera's sword, not Major Hawkins', would better symbolize the Western past. And one painting by an Indian who participated in the Battle of Little Bighorn would carry more historical weight than a dozen Remington cavalry charges.[61]

But what is to be done with the existing legacy? Historic sites have been selected to commemorate white civilization's progress westward. You can reinterpret the Custer Battlefield, renaming it the Little

Bighorn Battlefield National Monument, erecting a memorial to the Indian victors, making it more user friendly. But what about the scores of battlefields on which American troops emerged victorious? Will each become a monument to shame? And the trading posts and forts and missions and churches and ranches and factories, the landmarks on the trail west, the monuments to explorers and soldiers and railroad builders and town founders and pioneer families scattered across the west, honoring what was understood as a noble enterprise —must these, too, be passed by, with eyes averted, in embarrassed silence? What about the ruts still marking the paths emigrants made across the continent, their worldly belongings packed into wagons and carts, pulled by horses, mules, oxen, even by hand on a trek whose magnitude defies modern comprehension? One had to measure the journey in weeks and months, yet an instrument—a pendulum odometer—attached to a wagon's wheel translated revolutions into miles. It stands for the rational mind imposing limits on vastness, measuring progress to confirm the certainty of closure. It is also a poignant memento of the crossing.[62]

ABOVE
Wagon Pendulum Odometer
American, 1850s
Brass and leather
Strapped to the spoke of a wagon wheel, this
instrument converted the number of revolutions
to miles traveled.

Richard White has characterized the overland migration by the garbage left behind. The Oregon and California Trails were highways littered with abandoned goods and broken-down wagons and dead animals. No pristine wilderness here, just well-strewn trails through a well-used land. Greg MacGregor, a modern-day photographer, has followed the wagon ruts on the California Trail and leveled a realistic viewfinder on the Western experience. Today several significant sites on the route are still marked by litter—tire dumps, automobile graveyards, twentieth-century detritus. No romance here, either. Nevertheless, the author of an essay accompanying a selection of MacGregor's photographs concludes that even as we acknowledge the pioneers' "sexist inequalities, racist contempt for the people whose native land was being ravaged and taken away, cruelty to the long-suffering animals that pulled the wagons, destruction of the environment," we must not forget the sacrifices the trail represented. "Somehow it seems to me," Walter T. Anderson writes, "that if we are to disturb these ghosts at all, pay any mind to the piece of the past that is engraved out there in the soil and interred beneath the city streets, we need to do it with a mature, steady eye that neither romanticizes nor condemns."[63]

The four hundredth anniversary of Columbus' discovery of America was honored in countless ways in 1892-93, including a world's fair—the World Columbian Exposition—held in Chicago and devoted to the theme of Western development. The fair occasioned Turner's frontier thesis, an extended visit by Buffalo Bill's Wild West, and enough Indian sculpture to fill a hall. In stark contrast, the five hundredth anniversary of the same "discovery" (as it is now commonly rendered in deference to the native population already on hand and neither lost nor in need of being—to use Whitman's word— "found") was heavy on soul-searching repentance. Replacing the traditional triumphalist narrative of white pioneering progress in the nineteenth-century West will take time. A more inclusive West will come with what one historian has described as the "longer, grimmer, but more interesting story" that succeeds it. But an inclusive West will have to make room for the Old as well as the New, the mythic as well as the mundane—for comedy as well as tragedy.[64]

ESCAPE: AN ENDLESS PLACE

Early in 1872 George Catlin wrote to the New York papers to lay claim to an idea he had first expressed thirty years before which, he modestly explained, made him the progenitor of Yellowstone Park. Based on his observations on the Upper Missouri in 1832, he had remarked in his *Letters and Notes on the Manners, Customs, and Conditions of the North American Indians* (1841) on the certain fate awaiting Western nature. The buffalo, chased from their eastern range, now pastured exclusively on "the almost boundless prairies of the West" where, like the Indians who hunted them, they had fled "towards the 'setting sun.'" Soon, however, civilization would arrive and crowd the great herds to extinction. "What a splendid contemplation," he continued,

> *when one . . . imagines them as they might in future be seen, (by some great protecting policy of government) preserved in their pristine beauty and wildness, in a magnificent park, where the world could see for ages to come, the native Indian in his classic attire, galloping his wild horse, with sinewy bow, and shield and lance, amid the fleeting herds of elk and buffaloes. What a beautiful and thrilling specimen for America to preserve and hold up to the view of her refined citizens and the world, in future ages! A nation's Park, containing man and beast, in all the wild and freshness of their nature's beauty!*

Catlin was a born visionary. All he asked was that time itself be stopped forever. The Yellowstone Park bill before Congress in 1872 did not go quite that far. But in forwarding the extract from his book, Catlin offered a suggestion: "it will be seen that the writer contemplated the preservation of native men and native animals amidst the groves, the rocks and the ravines of native scenery; and it is to be hoped that, in the move being made in Congress these very proper embellishments to those picturesque scenes may not be left out."[65]

Yellowstone National Park, which defied Thomas Moran's initial attempt to express it conventionally, became the testing ground for many of the ideas underlying the national park system as it evolved in the twentieth century. The notion of preserving wilderness as a playground for the nation embraced contradictory impulses. It assumed that conquering the wilderness had run its course. Those who had labored to that end could now lay down their axes and string their hammocks between the trees left standing, glorying in a wilderness become scarce, and thus infinitely precious. But what should be preserved? Natural flora and fauna, certainly, though this would not be achieved without controversy. Westerners never stopped resisting game laws that denied them hunting rights, and it took the U.S. army to establish the inviolability of park borders. It makes for an arresting image: the boys in blue protecting nature against the forces of change and development. The continuing controversies surrounding park animals that have presumed to stray outside allotted borders indicate that even after a century and a quarter, the decision to preserve wildlife—from native buffalo to imported wolves—has complicated implications. Indeed, the concepts of wildlife and wilderness still seem foreign to some park visitors who recoil when nature wears a threatening face. Yellowstone Park has been sued for bear attacks, unwise plunges into geyser fields and hot pools, falls from precipices and other natural disasters. Apparently wilderness should be housebroken. Kill the bears for thinking they too have rights. Fence in every hot pool. Nature must be as benign as a Bierstadt painting if it wants to live out in the open, uncaged. But the most refractory contradiction in the national park ideal was one Catlin himself exposed. In drafting his letter to the press in 1872, he had originally written that Yellowstone should be "confined and protected within impassible boundaries,

LLOWSTONE – PARK

ABOVE
Poster for Yellowstone National Park
G. Schuh and Company, Munich, Germany
Lithograph on paper

Friend Harry

I received your letter
also picture of gun and red cote with sketch of old time
saddle and am much obliged
will be in your camp saterdy and we will talk it over
as a talker I am better than a green hand
but with the pen I am I am mere deaf and dumb
with regards to you and yours
Your friend
CM Russell

from which the ages to come might see and appreciate what once was the great Far West, and what the destructive and remodeling hands of civilization have done in turning the barren wilds into furrows and harvests of the plough." He must then have paused to reflect, recognizing a logical conundrum: nature to be preserved within impassable boundaries so that posterity could visit it as it once was. He deleted the passage, and sent the letter. But Catlin had identified the problem historian Roderick Nash addressed nearly a century later in observing that Americans, having learned to love their wilderness, were now in danger of loving it to death.[66]

Besides flora and fauna, was there room for indigenous peoples in the parks? After all, Indians, for so long considered synonymous with wild nature (the Indian/buffalo symbiosis), had tourist appeal as well. Once upon a time in the West, the frontier's reputation for crudity and violence was a bad thing, and respectable Eastern folks stayed far away, leaving it to reporters and illustrators to confirm their prejudices. But by the 1880s, with railroad lines crisscrossing the continent and all real danger removed, the West of Buffalo Bill and Roosevelt and Remington came to seem enticing. At that exact moment, railroad publicity stopped assuring potential passengers that the West was entirely safe for travelers and began assuring them that they would find it as wild and wooly as ever. Casting aside the allegorical tradition pitting nature against technology, Indians were heavily used to help sell tickets for railroad lines eager to attract tourists to the West. They were part of the publicity promoting every Western park. Of course, only a certain kind of Indian need apply. They must shuck off the civilized garb that was their everyday wear, and put on head bands, feather bonnets and buckskins to conform to tourist expecations. The future wanted representatives of the past, which did not mean allowing Indians to live within park boundaries and pursue present-day activities. That would be a violation of the pristine ideal.[67]

Tourists lured west by railroad propaganda at the beginning of the century hoped for an experience equivalent to the massive log hotels sprouting up in the wilderness parks, at once rustic and comfortable. What they were not prepared for was an adventure Yellowstone Park offered approximately once every ten years between 1887 and 1917: an old-fashioned stagecoach robbery. The passengers who crowded onto the coaches and carriages outside Old

OPPOSITE PAGE
Charles M. Russell (1864-1926)
Letter to Harry Stanford, 1912
Ink and watercolor on paper
Donated by George Montgomery

RIGHT
Charles M. Russell (1864-1926)
Standing Buffalo, ca. 1900-1920
Wax, plaster and paint
Donated by Mr. and Mrs. Gene Autry

Faithful Inn on August 24, 1908 had no inkling what was in store for them. Escorted by a cavalryman, the caravan of twenty-five conveyances, traveling about a hundred yards apart because of the dust, was surprised four and a half miles down the road by a lone highwayman armed with a repeating rifle who let the soldier and the first eight coaches pass, then stepped out of hiding and systematically robbed the rest of the procession. Just as the last flurry of outlawery in Wyoming titillated as much as it appalled, inspiring what is often regarded as the first Western motion picture, *The Great Train Robbery* (1903), a friend's account of being robbed in Yellowstone inspired Charlie Russell to make a pencil drawing of the holdup. The clock had not been merely stopped, its hands had been turned back. Now that was Wild Westing! Once the danger had passed the 152 victims immediately began exercising their bragging rights. On the evening of the robbery they held a formal meeting at the elegant Lake Hotel to record their losses and to commemorate the event with a brochure, *Souvenir List of the Yellowstone Park Holdup Victims of the Greatest Stage Coach Holdup and Robbery in the Twentieth Century*. Tourists were able to incorporate such experiences into a Western drama, as though the robbery had been staged just for their benefit. The last of the Yellowstone Park stage holdups took place in 1915.

Among the victims was Bernard Baruch, who quipped, "It was the best $50 I ever spent." Presumably the experience struck him as equivalent to riding on the Deadwood stagecoach at a performance of Buffalo Bill's Wild West—thrilling, noisy, and reasonably safe.[68]

What stirred Russell to depict the 1908 stagecoach robbery was a case of arrested development. The point of his art was stopping time: he could do on canvas and in sculpture what he only wished he could do in real life. Historical Western subjects occupied a single dimension—the past. But wildlife subjects belonged equally to past, present and future. On excursions from Bull Head Lodge, his home on Lake McDonald where he spent every summer, Russell could study "nature's cretures" undisturbed, since the area had been enclosed within the borders of Glacier National Park in 1910. He loved to model animals—buffalo and bear and wolves in particular—but his enthusiasm ran the gamut from skunks

OPPOSITE PAGE ABOVE
Charles M. Russell (1864-1926)
Wolf, ca. 1900-1920
Wax, plaster and paint
Donated by Mr. and Mrs. Gene Autry

OPPOSITE PAGE BELOW
Charles M. Russell (1864-1926)
Bighorn Sheep, ca. 1900-1920
Wax, plaster and paint
Donated by Mr. and Mrs. Gene Autry

ABOVE
Charles M. Russell (1864-1926)
Mountain Goat, ca. 1900-1920
Wax, plaster and paint
Donated by Mr. and Mrs. Gene Autry

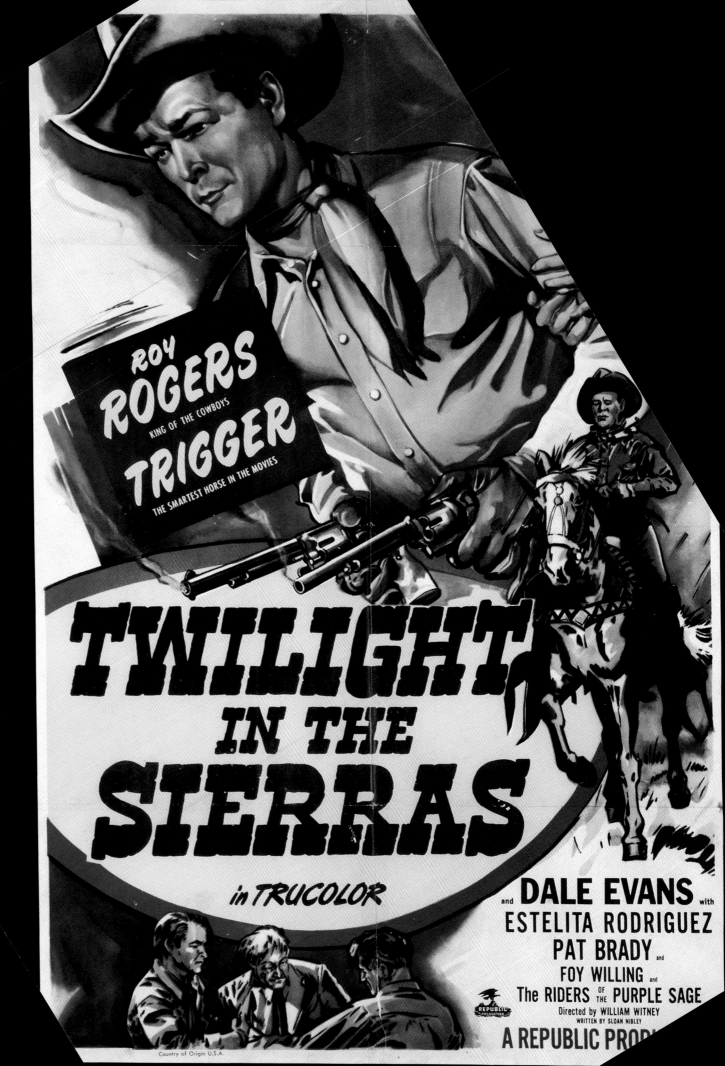

and porcupines to mountain goats and mountain sheep. A small watercolor showing a herd of buffalo on the move and a trailing wolf embellished a Russell letter in 1912. Its effortless expertise delighted the recipient, Harry Stanford, who made his living as a taxidermist stuffing animals and mounting trophy heads.

Practical considerations dictated that Russell paint hunting scenes in the twentieth century. They made good calendars for all the deskbound Walter Mittys who dreamed of adventure and escape. The West, such pictures promised, was still out there, awaiting them. Was there a hunting lodge or a sportsman's den that failed to display a Russell print or two? Russell did not hunt himself, but had no scruples about accompanying others on a hunting trip every autumn and eating his share of the venison and elk they killed. For him, hunting pictures showing men confronting animals in a wilderness setting created a bridge between the Old West and the present. His hunters were dressed in Western garb, rode horses, and breathed the tonic air of the great outdoors. Bear subjects were a favorite, since the match between armed man and powerful bruin seemed fair, and had such a venerable tradition in the frontier tales he had devoured as a boy. For Russell, hunting pictures solved the problem of suspending time.

Western art, Western fiction, Western film—all are created by individuals who use telephones, ride in cars, fly in airplanes, go to movies, watch television, type on word processors, surf the net. Yet the classic Western is devoid of reference to modern technology. B.M. Bower, a Russell friend with a huge readership that may or may not have realized she was a woman, defied convention in some of her early ranch romances (the first published in 1906) by setting them in the present and introducing such "unorthodox elements" as automobiles, airplanes, motion pictures and radio. By the thirties Bower, perhaps responsive to Depression times escapism, had dropped all reference to modern technology in her Western novels. But she had negotiated the exchange between past and present fundamental to understanding the Western, and Western myth, in the twentieth century. In popular culture the West remains a timeless neverneverland, outside the imperative of change. Guests reach dude ranches by plane and car; but the ranches cater to a yearning to get away from it all. It is as though, in traveling west through space, one can travel back in time. Introduce a horse and the out-of-doors, and you are there.[69]

Asked if a television series involving airplanes and set in the West would qualify as a Western, a student of TV Westerns demurred, only to be reminded that jeeps and trucks regularly appeared in the films and televisions shows of Gene Autry and Roy Rogers. The Western movie star, like Buffalo Bill before him, had two lives. In the 1870s, Buffalo Bill played himself on stage, then took to the field to be what he pretended to be. Forty years later, as an old man, he was still playing himself in a motion picture about his youthful deeds. The Western movie star was both a modern man and a screen persona. For his fans, however, the persona was the man. In the early years of film, Westerns blurred reality. Besides Buffalo Bill, historical figures like lawmen Bill Tilghman and Wyatt Earp, outlaws Al Jennings and Emmett Dalton, and the cowboy detective Charles A. Siringo also played bit roles, if not themselves. It was a matter of pride for Western stars like Tom Mix to insist upon their authentic credentials, too. Thus Mix was promoted as a former cowboy, rodeo performer, hunting guide, Rough Rider and law officer. "Four times desperately wounded," he still carried "three slugs in his body."

In the twenties, his fans might think of him riding his wonder horse Tony, but see him riding in one of his stable of expensive imported automobiles, its silver hood ornament showing Mix bulldogging a steer in tribute to the role that paid for everything. His only rival in popularity as a Western star at the time was his studio mate Buck Jones, a race car mechanic and cow puncher before he became a

ABOVE
Movie Poster for Riders of the Purple Sage
H.C. Miner Litho. Company, New York, 1925
Lithograph on paper

LEFT
Movie Poster for Western Luck
H.C. Miner Litho. Company, New York, 1924
Lithograph on paper

ABOVE
Movie still from *Gaucho Serenade*, 1940
From left to right: Smiley Burnett, Gene Autry,
Clifford Severn, Jr., June Storey (in wedding dress)
and Mary Lee. Courtesy of Gene Autry.

OPPOSITE PAGE ABOVE
Fritz Scholder (1937-)
Matinee Cowboy, Posing, 1978
Oil on canvas
*Donated by Fritz Scholder and
"Dedicated to my first hero, Monte Hale."*

OPPOSITE PAGE BELOW
Gallery Installation, Autry Museum of Western Heritage, 1997
Western themed toys and products of the early 1960s allowed
youngsters to play the roles of their favorite heroes of television
and the movies. No end of products bore the names of the
Lone Ranger, Roy Rogers, Hopalong Cassidy and others.

Hollywood stuntman and then a hero on the silver screen. "A true cowboy in every respect," according to publicity, Jones drove a Dusenberg sporting a silver steer head ornament.[70]

What followed when a child saw Gene Autry, Roy Rogers, Rex Allen or some other Western star alive, on stage or in the arena, playing the role of cowboy hero, was a conspiracy with the actor to suspend disbelief. His presence overrode the past; he existed in the here and now, and the West lived in him. You wanted to be Gene or Roy or Rex or Hoppy—not a cowboy, but a real cowboy, a matinee idol. And a bedroom full of monogrammed gear made you one when your cheek touched that special pillow at night. All the Western stars of the forties and fifties had comic books of their own that, like the dime novels of Buffalo Bill's day, gave their personas even more room to roam. "Comic-book cowboys could address contemporary social problems because of the anachronistic nature of their existence," William W. Savage, Jr., has observed:

> They went about on horseback and camped out at night and had to do with rather primitive Indians, but there was no historical context. They rode the mid-twentieth century West, among cars and trucks and planes and speedboats and all manner of modern technological wonders, suggesting that the mainstream meandered freely through the outback and that western social issues were merely American social issues writ rural.

And so you chased the owlhoots across that Western wasteland, dust rising, guns blazing, horses snorting, jeep engines revving, just as they always had.[71]

THEN WE CAME DOWN TO THE SEA

"We all know what birds of a feather do," Owen Wister remarks in *The Virginian*. "And it may be safely surmised that if a bird of any particular feather has been for a long while unable to see other birds of its kind, it will flock with them all the more assiduously when they happen to alight in its vicinity."[72]

At noon on March 19, 1924 Harry Carey picked Charlie Russell up at the house where he was staying in Los Angeles to drive him to the circus, feed him dinner, and generally keep him out of the way while Nancy made final preparations for his big birthday party that night. The guest list was impressive, including Will and Betty Rogers, the Careys, the actress Pauline Frederick, the novelist Gene Stratton Porter, the artists Edward Borein and Jack W. Smith, and the historian and writer Charles F. Lummis, a certified California character in his Spanish "suit of corduroy with a Hopi belt and an Indian drawn-work shirt and a white sombrero." Joe De Yong, Charlie's only protege, had accompanied the Russells to California grateful for "the chance to meet the people they knew." Besides Borein and Smith, he was introduced to such established Western painters as Maynard Dixon and Frank Tenney Johnson and the noted Western novelist B.M. Bower. He attended one of Lummis' famous "noises," a Saturday night gathering of some fifty people at El Alisal, the home Lummis built by hand that was, De Yong noted, "a common meeting ground for any one in this section who does any thing in Art, Literature or Music . . . . This place seems to be real Bohemia—" De Yong also established connections in Hollywood that paid off in his future career as costume designer and technical advisor for films ranging from *The Plainsman* (1936) to *Shane* (1953).[73]

In the early years of this century, when he was breaking into the Eastern market for illustrations and looking for galleries to handle his work, Russell met almost everybody in New York City who had a professional stake in the West—entertainers, writers, publishers and artists running the gamut from Will Rogers and William S. Hart to Charles Schreyvogel, Edward Borein, Edwin W. Deming and Frederic Remington. There were even more birds to flock with in Southern California in the 1920s, where the

movie industry lured old-time Westerners and big-time stars, and the whole galaxy of professional Westerners who had come to share in the good fortune. As it had since the gold rush, California still exerted an irresistible pull. In 1924 the Russells were making their fifth consecutive visit. Los Angeles had grown by at least 100,000 people since the last

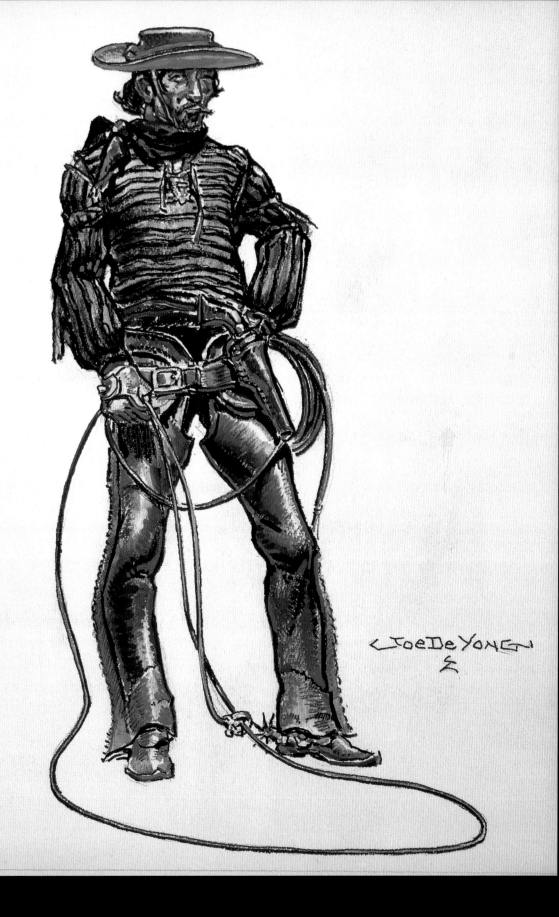

102

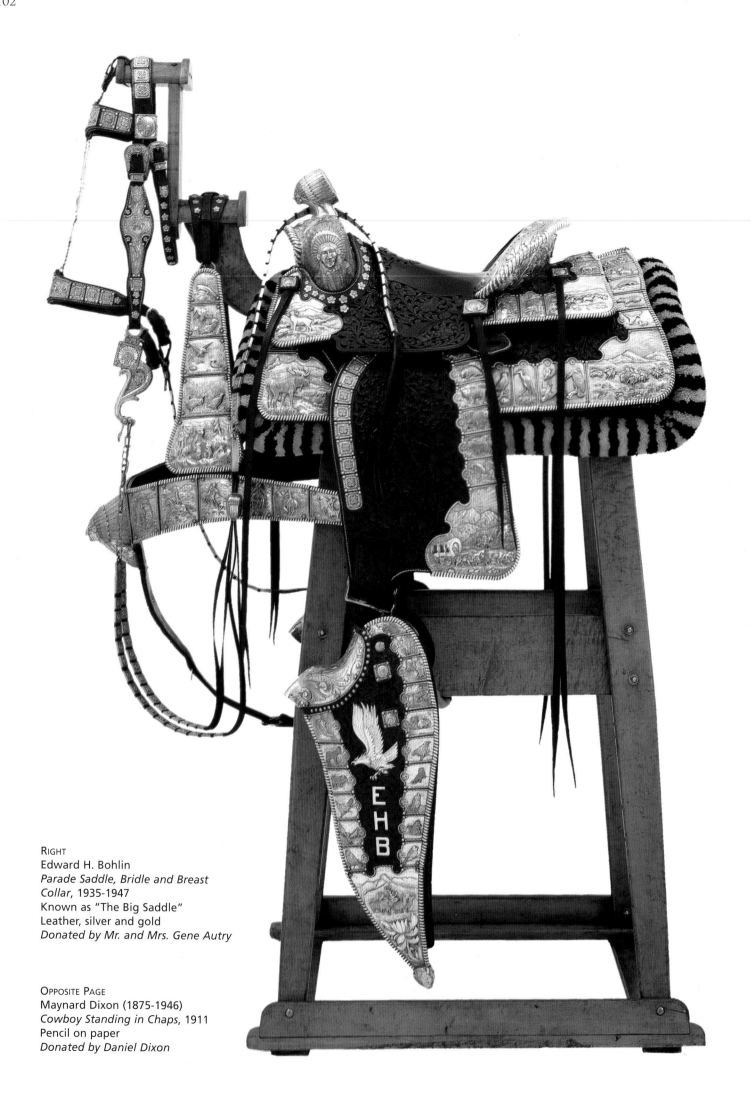

time they saw it, and was lurching towards one million—or was already there. No one knew for sure. It was said that a million tourists visited annually, and perhaps as many as 150,000 stayed. Where else was there to go?—the West had hit the sea.[74]

Charlie Russell's first impression of Southern California was that "its strictly man made." But he loved Western movies, and relished watching Tom Mix, William S. Hart and Will Rogers at work. The gun-toting characters they played were all "to fancyfull to be real but to an old romance loving boy like me its the best thing Iv seen in Calif." As he would each time he went south, Russell visited the Harry Carey Ranch, 3,700 acres in the San Fernando Valley about forty miles north of Los Angeles, to observe Harry, his wife Olive, and her younger sister Mignonne Golden make Westerns. And he complained about the weather: "We are camped now in a bunglow at Pasadena among flowers and palm trees that have been here long enough not to mind the cold ore maby the flowers are like the native sons they wont admit it."[75]

In 1921 the Russells stayed in Los Angeles. Charlie saw Will Rogers often and made the acquaintance of Douglas Fairbanks and Mary Pickford, who would become patrons of his art. "Heres to history and romance and you and your kind," Russell wrote in a fan letter, "men and women who make folkes of history and story bookes live and breath again." Charlie also visited Neal Hart and Buck Conners, both active in the movies, and complained about the weather. The next year the Russells returned to Pasadena. Charlie socialized with Lummis, "A Scout that back trackes Dim trails," recognizing in

him a kindred spirit whose Spanish outfits were no more eccentric than his own boots, sash and Stetson, and visited old friends as well as making new ones including the writers Eugene Manlove Rhodes and Henry H. Knibbs. And he complained about the weather.[76]

In 1923 the Russells stayed in Santa Barbara. Charlie sold several paintings at healthy prices, and complained about the weather. But that year Nancy bought the lot in Pasadena next to her father's. Nineteen twenty-four found the Russells back in California—living with friends in Los Angeles, then on their own in Pasadena. Besides all the mixing at the Lummis soiree and his own birthday party, Russell renewed his acquaintance with two transplanted

LOUIS WEISS
presents

HARRY **CAREY**
IN

"BORDER DEVILS"

WITH **KATHLEEN COLLINS** • NILES WELCH
GEORGE HAYES • AL SMITH
OLIVE FULLER GOLDEN • MERRILL McCORMICK
MASTON WILLIAMS • RAY GALLAGHER

DIRECTED BY
WILLIAM NIGH
STORY BY
MURRAY LEINSTER
PRODUCTION MGR.
GEO. M. MERRICK
SETTINGS BY
TEC ART STUDIOS, INC.
PRODUCED BY
SUPREME FEATURES, INC., LTD.
ALFRED T. MANNON, PRES.
DISTRIBUTED BY
WEISS BROS. ARTCLASS
PICTURES CORP.

BARBWIRE

WALT COBURN

Montanans, George T. Browne, once a saloon keeper in Cut Bank, Great Falls and Butte and now a successful Los Angeles realtor, and Walt Coburn, a prolific Western story writer. Charlie was silent about the California weather but loud about his preference for Montana. There was never much doubt why.

Walt Coburn was a consummate professional. He knew the formula for successful pulp fiction Westerns, and he adhered to it: "they want lots of riding, shooting, gore-wading yarns and in order to keep the pr[o]verbial wolf from the proverbial door, I give it to em—with trimmings." Sentiment never clouded his shrewd calculation of the market. Teddy Blue Abbott summed up the world of Westerns with the succinct observation that "an old hand knows dam well" they "are 95 Per Cent lies and the other 5 Per Cent (B.S.)." Walt Coburn was an unblinking realist; his older half-brother Wallace, a close friend of Russell's in their wild oats days, twinned himself with the "Cowboy Artist" as the "Cowboy Poet" and in 1899 published a collection of rangeland verse, illustrated by Russell, under the title *Rhymes from a Round-Up Camp*. As sentimental as his brother was clear-eyed, Wallace in 1917 dedicated a poem, "Passing Trails," to C. M. Russell:

> The plowshare cuts the cattle trails
>> Where trod the long-horn steers,
> And memory holds in cherished store
>> The wealth of by-gone years . . . .

>> Trail-herds are dreams of early days,
>>> The buffalo have died,
>> And dry farms dot the coulees
>>> Where the grey wolf used to hide . . . .

>> I'm tired of twenty story shacks,
> Of cars and jitney things;
>> The music of the cabarets
> No pleasure to me brings . . . .

> So let me dream of a wilder west,
>> A country fresh and new
> And when I'm through, I hope I'll ride
>> To the land of the Buckaroo.

OPPOSITE PAGE ABOVE
Edward Borein
Roping a Steer, ca. 1938
Watercolor on paper

OPPOSITE PAGE BELOW
Frank Tenney Johnson
Changing Horses on the Pony Express, 1927
Oil on canvas

ADOLPH ZUKOR AND JESSE L. LASKY
PRESENT
An IRVIN WILLAT Production
NORTH OF 36
with JACK HOLT
ERNEST TORRENCE
LOIS WILSON & NOAH BEERY
FROM THE FAMOUS NOVEL BY
EMERSON HOUGH
SCREEN PLAY BY JAMES HAMILTON
a Paramou
PRODUCED BY FAMOUS

Sentiment of the same sort prompted Russell in March 1924 to write a letter to *Adventure Magazine* protesting an attack on the novelist Emerson Hough for falsifying history in his trail-driving novel *North of 36*. Citing Teddy Blue as his main authority, Russell debated the critic point by point. His most revealing

defense, however, was personal: "Hough looked for romance mixen it with History he rote storyes I liked."[77]

Romance shaped Russell's brand of realism; and realism shaped Walt Coburn's brand of romance. Westerns were a business, and Hollywood the factory that produced them for the screen. Western writers and Western actors flocked to the coast because that is where the business was: the dream of westering had become Dream Factory fodder.[78]

Charlie did not accompany Nancy down to Los Angeles in the spring of 1925, but in 1926 they stayed in Hollywood, "the largest moovie camp in the world," and the movies still provided an inexhaustible topic for comment: "thair are more two gun men here now than the history of the west from north to south ever knew . . . if the old west had of been as tough as the mooves make it thayd be runing buffalo yet on the Great Falls flat." Nancy's plans to build a home on their lot in Pasadena were moving forward. California friends had been shaken by a serious earthquake in the Santa Barbara area the previous year, and Charlie used it to advantage in his campaign to stay put in Great Falls. "This is a nice country," he granted, "but like any other old hoss, I like my old range best. Right now I wouldn't trade any part of Arrow Creek for the best they have got here. California is shure the picnic ground of this country but I only like picnics a short time." He died that October.[79]

Montana was always the real West to Russell, but California had forced him to expand his definition. The West was wherever the old days lived on. A visit to Mexico in 1906 and the Grand Canyon country in 1916 had brought the Southwest into the range of his personal experience, and he told Ed Borein, artist to artist, "If I savyed the south west like you Id shure paint Navys [Navajos]":

> it was at a little lake in the desert at sun down a bunch of these
> American Arabs droped down from the high country with about five
> hundred horses most of these riders looked lik the real thing in there
> high forked saddles and concho belts silver are turquois necklaces and
> year [ear] rings . . . They were not like the Indians I know but every
> thing on them spelt wild people and horsemen and in a mixture of dust
> and red sunlight it made a picture that will not let me foget Arizona

The Southwest would never lack for painters specializing in Indians, scenery, or both. Jimmy Swinnerton, a successful cartoonist who met Russell and knew Borein and Dixon well, began exhibiting his desert landscapes in San Francisco and Los Angeles in 1921. Russell believed that "a picture is not a picture without figures in it." However, the vivid colors of Swinnerton's *Corrals in Hopi Land*, where hot tones play off cobalt blue, realize the spirit of Russell's evocative word picture ("dust and red sunlight"), if not its particulars.

Swinnerton was characterized in one review as "a self-appointed publicity agent for the great American Desert"; for Russell, the West was never just a place, but a place in time.[80]

— THE THINKER —

When Russell waxed eloquent about California scenery ("roling country green with patches of poppies and live Oak mountian ranges with white peaks that streach away to no where"), it was as "fine back ground for cow pictures." He lamented the fact that California artists settled for landscapes instead of painting "the history of the State." To Will James

OPPOSITE PAGE ABOVE
William T. Ranney
Hunting Wild Horses, 1846
Oil on canvas

OPPOSITE PAGE BELOW
S. Loomis, Santa Barbara, California
California Saddle, 1881
Leather, wood and steel

BELOW
Trade Sign for "J.C. Johnson and Co."
San Francisco, California
Lithograph on paper, ca. 1880

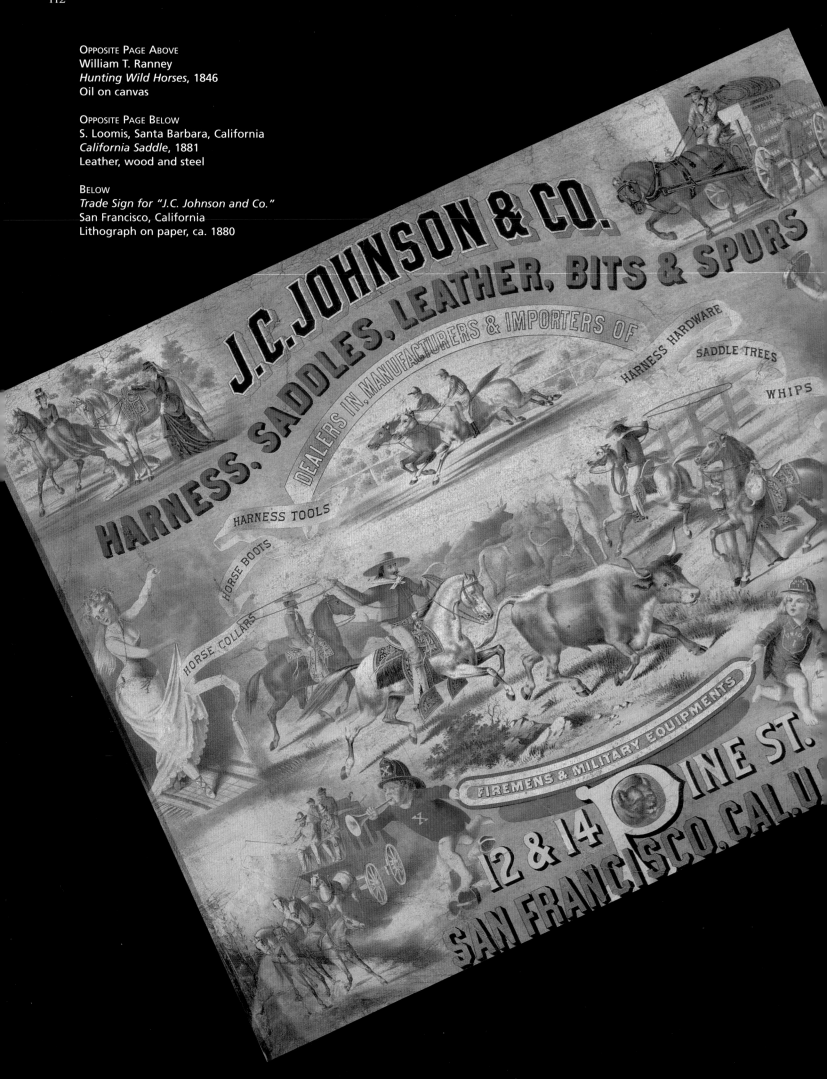

he wrote: "I have never seen this kind of country used in cow pictures Why dont you try it If I knew more about that country Id shure go after it its full of cow history Califonia was a cow range before those Good Puritan Fathers stole what is now New England from the Inguns on the East coast."

California was authentic, then, even if Will James was not. Born Ernest Dufault in St. Nazaire d'Acton, Quebec, he had reinvented himself as a Montana-born cowboy, and put his dreams on paper as author and illustrator of such rangeland classics as *Smoky, the Cowhorse*, published in 1926. That same year, Russell got to see buckaroos brand about 1,000 calves on his cousin's ranch near Hollister, and was thoroughly impressed:

> *Saw some good roping and they rode good horses these Buckarues*
> *are more like the cow punchers of long ago than aney Iv seen*
> *they still use senter fire saddels and a raw hide ropes most of*
> *them use raw hide ranes and thair all dally men maby they cant work as*
> *fast as tie men but they shure do thair work pritty*

That was the picture California offered the Western artist. Not pretty poppies, but pretty cowpunching. Not landscape, but good horses and good roping—five words that define Charlie Russell's West.[81]

But what, in popular opinion, was the West? A writer in 1920 rephrased it "Is there a West?," and after a train journey to California on which he spotted only three prairie-dogs and "one superannuated cowboy of about eighty," concluded that the Old West of Buffalo Bill had become "shadowy and elusive." "The West, if it exists, has already been pushed beyond the High Sierras. It only remains to discover whether or not it has been shoved into the Pacific and safely out of American life." The definitions of the West offered by Jefferson, Pine and Roosevelt in the nineteenth century had run out of room in the twentieth. California was it, or there was no West. This put a heavy burden on California as the last hope for all the hopes that westering inspired. Could human happiness prove as changeless as the climate, and everlasting? Would serenity suffice?[82]

Miners: A Moment at Rest (1882) by Ernest Narjot is, at once, a history painting (the scene was set some thirty years before) and a genre piece—"genrefied history," to borrow a phrase. It portrays domestic tranquility in an all-male world. No horse-racing, drinking or high jinks break the spell. No Wild West. Instead, Narjot offers a sentimental portrait of California pioneer life defined by . . . niceness. Could that be the sum total of all the struggle and sacrifice and dreaming? Cross a continent for a place in the sun to read the newspaper, a contented dog at one's feet? No hunger still gnawing at the restless heart? West-fever extinguished by salt water? In his corrosive masterpiece The Day of the Locust (1939), Nathanael West projected the moment after the moment at rest. What happens, he asked, when the Iowans who have staked their all on the California Dream reach California? They craved not betterment, but transformation; not a nice place to spend a drowsy Sunday afternoon, but an earthly paradise. What they got instead were oranges and sunsets. They can eat just so many oranges, watch only so many suns dip hissing into the swells. "Their boredom becomes more and more terrible," West writes. "They realize that they've been tricked and burn with resentment." They had "come to California to die," confident of a happy ending. But in coming to California and living out their dreams, they had outlived their dreams. There was nowhere else for them to go. "Any dream was better than no dream," West warns; now a happy ending was denied them forever.[83]

And still they came. For professional Westerners—artists, writers, actors—Los Angeles in the twenties was a magnet. For old-time Westerners, according to the daughter of a cowboy stunt rider, it was an "unofficial Burial Ground of the Elephants." She was thinking of Major Gordon W. Lillie (Pawnee Bill), Buffalo Bill's one-time partner, and Wyatt Earp and the outlaw Al Jennings—and Charlie Russell. They all crowded together on that mythic shore. "Los Angeles has touched the imagination of America," a 1923 promotional tract boasted: "She has become an idea . . . a longing in men's breasts. . . . She is the symbol of a new civilization, a new hope, another TRY of ambition." Los Angeles was, in short, the Western myth reborn. To justify its title "The World's Greatest City," the tract included an anecdote about two American soldiers in Paris dreaming of a better city back home: "I'm going to dust off the old flivver and beat it for out West . . . I just came out of a movie and it showed Hollywood and real human beings and mountains and some American gals and everything . . . . Oh, Guy, there's where this bird is going to set purty with Riley!"[84]

ABOVE
Ernest Narjot (1827-1898)
Miners: A Moment at Rest (Gold Rush Camp), 1882
Oil on canvas

They were impressive characters, those old-time Westerners, with their ability to cross rivers and continents in memories that cancelled the line between past and present. "I run across Lum Reid last week in town," Teddy Blue Abbott wrote Charlie Russell from Gilt Edge, Montana, on February 1, 1926, where he still ranched nearly half a century after trailing a herd of cattle north from Texas. "We sure did have a visit," crossing "the river at Great Falls with that herd of 72 Beef. in fact we cross that herd every time we meet." Writing to Ed Borein from Hollywood six weeks later, Russell reported on a get-together with William Hawks, an Easterner who lived for his days as a rancher in Idaho in the nineties, and Charles Siringo, author of the first cowboy autobiography and a controversial Pinkerton detective. Hawks "has grown older," Russell commented, "but aint slowed up non on talk he was here the other day with Charley Ceringo and we shure rode and killed some betwine correll dust and smoke we almost choked." The dust of chases past . . . the pursuer, not mere mortals but time itself. When he could still make Western movies, William S. Hart recalled, he would hear the faint sound of the director's voice coming through the clouds of dust, "'Okay, Bill, Okay. Glad you made it . . . . Give old Fritz a pat on the nose for me, will you?' Oh, the thrill of it all!"[85]

They had come down to the ocean, these old West-dreamers, "like sea birds in mating time," drifting about "in a sort of delirium." Flocking to Sunset Land. They had sailed like the tawny hawks to "the edge of the world," where there was "only sun and sky":

> *The glowing, fire-eyed sun*
> *In glory dies in the west;*
> *And the bird with dreamy crest,*
> *And soft, sun-loving breast,*
> *When throbbing day is done,*
> *Floats slowly into the west.*

"Oh, Guy, there's where this bird is going to set purty . . ."

West-fever.

[1]   *Continental Monthly* 1 (March 1862): 246

[2]   C. M. Russell to Jim Thornhill, January 23, 1924, Nancy C. Russell typescript, Helen E. and Homer E. Britzman Collection, Taylor Museum for Southwestern Studies of the Colorado Springs Fine Arts Center (hereafter, Britzman); C. M. Russell to Philip R. Goodwin, April 10, 1920, *Charles M. Russell, Word Painter: Letters, 1887-1926*, Brian W. Dippie, ed. (Fort Worth: Amon Carter Museum, distributed by Harry N. Abrams, New York, 1993), p. 298; Joe De Yong to Mary De Yong, February 17, 1924, Joe De Yong Papers, National Cowboy Hall of Fame and Western Heritage Center, Oklahoma City; and see Brian W. Dippie, "Charlie Russell Meets California," *Montana: The Magazine of Western History* 34 (Summer 1984): 62-79.

[3]   C. M. Russell to Joseph G. Scheuerle, May 1, 1924, *Word Painter*, p. 350; Joe De Yong to Mary De Yong, February 17, 1924, De Yong Papers.

[4]   C. M. Russell to Richard Jones, February 8, 1923, *Word Painter*, p. 329; Irvin S. Cobb, *Roughing It De Luxe* (New York: George H. Doran, 1914), p. 97.

[5]   C. M. Russell to Philip R. Goodwin, April 10, 1920, *Word Painter*, p. 298. Robert G. Athearn, *The Mythic West in Twentieth-Century America* (Lawrence: University Press of Kansas, 1986), p. 20, identified this "Real West" as the Mountain West, "to distinguish it from the Middle West, on the one side, and the Far West on the other. In any case, if one accepts the argument that Americans chose to think of it as their last West, in historic terms, it is at least possible to identify this fugitive phenomenon in an emotional, if not completely a geographic, sense. Not infrequently, . . . the emotional became the physical." Also see Earl Pomeroy, *The Pacific Slope: A History of California, Oregon, Washington, Idaho, Utah, and Nevada* (New York: Alfred A. Knopf, 1965), p. 3, which opens: "The Pacific slope is both the most Western and, after the East itself, the most Eastern part of America. No other section is more like the Atlantic seaboard and Western Europe; no part is more different; and no part has wished more to be both."

[6]   Wallace Stegner, "Born a Square—The Westerners' Dilemma," *Atlantic Monthly* 213 (January 1964): 48; and, for a range of opinions, see Walter Nugent, "Where Is the American West?: Report on a Survey," *Montana: The Magazine of Western History* 42 (Summer 1992): 2-23.

[7]   Thomas Jefferson to William Ludlow, September 6, 1824, *The Writings of Thomas Jefferson*, Andrew A. Lipscomb and Albert Ellery Bergh, eds., 20 vols. (Washington, D.C.: Thomas Jefferson Memorial Association, 1903), XVI: 74-75; Thomas Jefferson to Horatio Gates, July 11, 1803, in Richard Skolnik, *1803: Jefferson's Decision: The United States Purchases Louisiana* (New York: Chelsea House, 1969), p. 155. The best history remains William H. Goetzmann, *Exploration and Empire: The Explorer and the Scientist in the Winning of the American West* (New York: Alfred A. Knopf, 1966), a book equal to its subject.

[8]   George W. Pine, *Beyond the West* (Utica: T. J. Griffiths, 2nd ed., 1871), pp. iii, 44-45.

[9]   Theodore Roosevelt, *The Winning of the West*, 6 vols. (New York: Current Literature Publishing, 1905 [1889-96]), VI: 239.

[10]   Henry David Thoreau, "A Week on the Concord and Merrimack Rivers" (1849), in *Walden and Other Writings of Henry David Thoreau*, Brooks Atkinson, ed. (New York: Modern Library College Editions, 1950), pp. 409-10; Leslie A. Fiedler and Arthur Zeiger, eds., *O Brave New World: American Literature from 1600 to 1840* (New York: Dell, 1968), p. 273; George Catlin, *Letters and Notes on the Manners, Customs, and Condition of the North American Indians*, 2 vols. (New York: Wiley and Putnam, 1841), I: 62. We will always see the West through someone's eyes—and we can always go precursor hunting. The point is that beginning points are hard to establish. Tearing up roots, the Western historian Bernard DeVoto learned, exposes root systems that take you farther back in time.

The third volume in his epic trilogy on Western history—*The Year of Decision* (1943), *Across the Wide Missouri* (1947) and *The Course of Empire* (1952)—continued his march backwards in time, from the pivotal year of 1846 to the heyday of the mountain men in the 1830s, to the Louisiana Purchase and the inauguration of what Roosevelt called Far Western history. In fact, *The Course of Empire* ended with the Lewis and Clark Expedition, where DeVoto had intended to begin it. In 1950 he wrote, "what annoys me is that so objective—well, that's what we gravely say—a thing as history should have its processes so deep and hidden in the unconscious. I had written—because it turned out I must—almost exactly 100,000 words when I reached the place where I originally thought the thing began . . . . I like small periods of time—this one deals in detail with two centuries, and just for the hell of it drops back to 700 A.D. and back of that to the ice age." Beyond that DeVoto defended, absolutely, American history as "the most romantic of all histories. It began in myth and has developed through centuries of fairy stories. Whatever the time is in America it is always, at every moment, the mad and wayward hour . . . Ours is a story mad with the impossible, it is by chaos out of dream, it began as dream and it has continued as dream down to the last headlines you read in a newspaper. And of our dreams there are two things above all others to be said, that only madmen could have dreamed them or would have dared to—and that we have shown a considerable faculty for making them come true." Bernard DeVoto, quoted in Edith R. Mirrielees, "The Writer," and in Catherine Drinker Bowen, "The Historian," in *Four Portraits and One Subject: Bernard DeVoto* (Boston: Houghton Mifflin, 1963), pp. 37-8, 25. Objections to DeVoto's triumphalism—perhaps inherent in narrative history where story must move towards resolution, and higher lessons emerge from the toil of individuals—are addressed in two essays by Lewis H. Lapham inspired by a symposium marking the centennial of DeVoto's birth: "Alms for Oblivion," *Harper's Magazine* 294 (March 1997): 9-11, and "The Spanish Armadillo," *Harper's Magazine* 294 (April 1997): 8, 10-11. Reflecting on "the differences between DeVoto's language—rooted in fact and grounded in narrative—and our own postliterate drift of images set to the music of television," Lapham makes a point that is broadly relevant to understanding the (occasionally) goofy presentism of some historical writing today: "The past is constantly dissolving into the eternal present, and the time is always now." A reviewer, "disappointed if not shocked" by evidence of racial prejudice in *The Papers of Will Rogers* for the years 1879-1904, warned that "most readers will not find everything here attractive"—as though the past *should* be attractive (Davis D. Joyce, review in the *Journal of American History* 84 [June 1997]: 266-67). Or consider this prefatory statement in a recent work of nineteenth-century art history by Angela Miller, *The Empire of the Eye: Landscape Representation and American Cultural Politics, 1825-1875* (Ithaca: Cornell University Press, 1993), p. 19: "There are . . . other aspects of my method for which I have less apparent justification in the material itself. I bring along the peculiar concerns of my own generation, a special way of seeing things that may make me appear at times to be discussing a very different body of work from that which has been the subject of previous studies. For I am of a generation of scholars that is constitutionally skeptical of self-justifying claims, that is inclined to discover multiple and often competing motives where our predecessors took things at face value," etc. "My generation" is a rock anthem, not a valid scholarly postulate. Given such attitudes, there can be no history.

11   F. Scott Fitzgerald, *The Great Gatsby* (New York: Charles Scribner's Sons, 1925), pp. 177, 100, 111, 182. And backwards we go, with Fitzgerald's concluding line: "So we beat on, boats against the current, borne back ceaselessly into the past." Wallace Stegner provided a definition of the Westerner almost touching in its tough love tenderness: "In a time of repudiation, absurdity, guilt, and despair, he still half believes in the American dream." Echoing Fitzgerald, Stegner offers an admonition—"Do not go back into history"—and hope: "while the West is admitting its inadequacy, let it remember its strength: it is the New World's last chance to be something better, the only American society still malleable enough to be formed" ("Born a Square—The Westerners' Dilemma," pp. 46-50). Forward looking, brave even while dragging the deadweight of the past—a burden of cynicism enough to over-whelm the hardiest optimist—the Westerner must struggle on believing (or at least half-believing) in the American Dream. In *Angle of Repose* (1971), Stegner struck a balance between hard-eyed realism and the romance of the West. It is the story of a gifted Eastern woman married to a mining engineer whose work in the last quarter of the nine-teenth-century takes them to California, Dakota, Colorado, Mexico and Idaho. She clings to the past, impervious to the West's appeal; he is a born dreamer, responsive to the land. Isolated and lonely, her cruel fate was to be "adrift in the hopeless West." "His clock was set on pioneer time. He met trains that had not yet arrived, he waited on platforms that hadn't yet been built, beside tracks that might never be laid . . . . Hope was always out ahead of fact, possibility obscured the outlines of reality" (*Angle of Repose* [New York: Fawcett Crest, 1971], pp. 445, 341).

For all he qualified his Western hopes, Stegner never abandoned them. See the introduction to the collection of essays published shortly before his death, *Where the Bluebird Sings to the Lemonade Springs: Living and Writing in the West* (New York: Random House, 1992). The title alone, "In the Big Rock Candy Mountains," is enough to establish the romantic ever lurking inside the realist.

[12]   O. E. Rolvaag, *Giants in the Earth: A Saga of the Prairie* (New York: Harper & Brothers, 1927), pp. 227, 464-65.

[13]   Willa Cather, *O Pioneers!* (Boston: Houghton Mifflin, 1962 [1913]), pp. 65, 48, 301, 308.

[14]   Wallace Stegner, *The Big Rock Candy Mountain* (New York: Sagamore Press, 1957 [1943]), pp. 458, 460-61; A. B. Guthrie, Jr., *The Way West* (Toronto: George J. McLeod, 1949), p. 337.

[15]   Cormac McCarthy, *Blood Meridian; or, The Evening Redness in the West* (New York: Vintage Books, 1992 [1985]), pp. 78, 285, 304.

[16]   Larry McMurtry, *Lonesome Dove* (New York: Simon and Schuster, 1985), pp. 81, 565, 786.

[17]   John Steinbeck, *The Red Pony* (New York: Bantam Books, 1963 [1937]), p. 91; A.B. Guthrie, Jr., *The Big Sky* (New York: William Sloane Associates, 1947), p. 385.

[18]   McMurtry, *Lonesome Dove*, p. 841; C. M. Russell to Edward "Kid" Price, June 1, 1917, *Word Painter*, p. 235.

[19]   C. M. Russell to E. C. "Teddy Blue" Abbott, October 4, 1923, Montana Historical Society, Helena; C. M. Russell to Charles A. Beil, May 31, 1926, *Word Painter*, pp. 393-94.

[20]   Charles M. Russell, "The Story of the Cowboy," *Montana Newspasper Association Insert*, November 1916; *Theodore Roosevelt: An Autobiography* (New York: Macmillan Company, 1913), p. 94. Written at the end of 1908, "The Story of the Cowboy" appeared in Russell's *Trails Plowed Under* (New York: Doubleday, Page, 1927) as "The Story of the Cowpuncher."

[21]   R. D. Warden, *CMRussell Boyhood Sketchbook* (Bozeman: Treasure Products, 1972).

[22]   Paul Fees, "In Defense of Buffalo Bill: A Look at Cody in and of His Time," in Chris Bruce, et al., *Myth of the West* (New York: Rizzoli, for the Henry Art Gallery, University of Washington, Seattle, 1990), p. 146. Also see *Buffalo Bill and the Wild West* (Pittsburgh: University of Pittsburgh Press, for the Brooklyn Museum, 1981) and Joseph G. Rosa and Robin May, *Buffalo Bill and His Wild West: A Pictorial Biography* (Lawrence: University Press of Kansas, 1989). The standard biography remains Don Russell, *The Lives and Legends of Buffalo Bill* (Norman: University of Oklahoma Press, 1960).

[23]   Charles M. Russell, "Hunting and Trapping on the Judith with Jake Hoover; When Lonely Trading Post Stood on Site of Lewistown," *Montana Newspaper Association Insert*, June 1917.

[24]   Fees, "In Defense of Buffalo Bill," p. 141.

[25]   Rosa and May, *Buffalo Bill and His Wild West*, reproduces several striking photographs of what Paul Fees has called the "Flamboyant Fraternity"; also see Darlis A. Miller, *Captain Jack Crawford: Buckskin Poet, Scout, and Showman* (Albuquerque: University of New Mexico Press, 1993), and Joseph G. Rosa, *Wild Bill Hickok: The Man and His Myth* (Lawrence: University Press of Kansas, 1996).

26   Russell, *Lives and Legends of Buffalo Bill*, pp. 231-32; and Paul L. Hedren, *First Scalp for Custer: The Skirmish at Warbonnet Creek, Nebraska, July 17, 1876* (Glendale, CA: Arthur H. Clark, 1980).

27   John Palliser, *Solitary Rambles and Adventures of a Hunter in the Prairies* (Edmonton: M. G. Hurtig, 1969 [1853]), pp. 230-34, 243. This replicates the Western experiences of Lewis and Clark and others, whose preferences yielded to buckskin practicalities once imported clothing wore out.

28   Willa Cather, *My Antonia* (Boston: Houghton, Mifflin, 1918), pp. 14-16.

29   Wayne Fields, foreword, and Joni L. Kinsey, *Plain Pictures: Images of the American Prairies* (Washington, DC: Smithsonian Institution Press, for the University of Iowa Museum of Art, 1996), pp. x-xvi, 5-6, *passim.*; and Nicolai Cikovsky, Jr., "'The Ravages of the Axe': The Meaning of the Tree Stump in Nineteenth-Century American Art," *Art Bulletin* 61 (December 1979): 611-26.

30   See, for example, the selection of illustrations reproduced in Lucius Beebe and Charles Clegg, *The American West: The Pictorial Epic of a Continent* (New York: E. P. Dutton, 1955).

31   Catlin, *Letters and Notes*, II: 3; I: 59; Palliser, *Solitary Rambles*, pp. 87, 106. For Stanley and Catlin, see Brian W. Dippie, *Catlin and His Contemporaries: The Politics of Patronage* (Lincoln: University of Nebraska Press, 1990); and for an appealing sample of Catlin's work, see Joan Carpenter Troccoli, *First Artist of the West: George Catlin Paintings and Watercolors from the Collection of Gilcrease Museum* (Tulsa: Gilcrease Museum, 1993).

32   Richard J. Huyda, *Camera in the Interior, 1858—H. L. Hime, Photogapher, The Assiniboine and Saskatchewan Exploring Expedition* (Toronto: Coach House Press, 1975), plates 44, 32; Cather, *My Antonia*, p. 5. No artist before Hime, Martha A. Sandweiss observes, "provided such a vivid image of the harsh, terrifying emptiness that awaited the western adventurer." ("Views and Reviews: Western Art and Western History," in *Under an Open Sky: Rethinking America's Western Past*, William Cronon, George Miles, and Jay Gitlin, eds. [New York: W. W. Norton, 1992], p. 194.)

33   Wallace Stegner, quoted in Thurman Wilkins, *Thomas Moran: Artist of the Mountains* (Norman: University of Oklahoma Press, 1966), p. 58. Moran has been fortunate in his scholarly commentators, for example, Carol Clark, *Thomas Moran: Watercolors of the American West* (Austin: University of Texas Press, 1980); William H. Goetzmann and William N. Goetzmann, *The West of the Imagination* (New York: W.W. Norton, 1986), chaps. 15-16; Anne R. Morand, Joni L. Kinsey and Mary Panzer, *Splendors of the American West: Thomas Moran's Art of the Grand Canyon and Yellowstone* (Birmingham: Birmingham Museum of Art, 1990) (p. 30 reproduces his 1870 conception of *Canon of the Yellowstone*); Anne Morand, *Thomas Moran: The Field Sketches, 1856-1923* (Norman: University of Oklahoma Press, for the Thomas Gilcrease Institute of American History and Art, Tulsa, 1996) (his earlier landscape sketches, pp. 28-30, merit comparison to his *Canon of the Yellowstone*); and Joni Louise Kinsey, *Thomas Moran and the Surveying of the American West* (Washington, DC: Smithsonian Institution Press, 1992).

34   Nancy K. Anderson and Linda S. Ferber, *Albert Bierstadt: Art & Enterprise* (New York: Hudson Hills Press, in association with the Brooklyn Museum, 1990); Kinsey, *Thomas Moran*, pp. 48, 89, and especially chap. 8 for an excellent discussion of *Mountain of the Holy Cross*.

35   Frederic Remington Diary, July 30, 1909, Frederic Remington Art Museum, Ogdensburg, NY; and see Donald J. Hagerty, *Desert Dreams: The Art and Life of Maynard Dixon* (Layton, UT: Gibbs Smith, 1993).

36   Frederick Jackson Turner, "The Significance of the Frontier in American History," *Annual Report of the American Historical Association for the Year 1893* (Washington, DC: Government Printing Office, 1894), pp. 199, 226-27.

37   Henry David Thoreau, Civil Disobedience," *Walden and Other Writings*, p. 645; F. P. Livingston, "The Great Scout," in *Life and Adventures of "Buffalo Bill" (Colonel William F. Cody)* (Chicago: Charles C. Thompson, 1917), p. iv.

[38]   Owen Wister, *The Virginian: A Horseman of the Plains* (New York: Macmillan, 1902), pp. viii, 9, 130; and see Lawrence R. Borne, *Dude Ranching: A Complete History* (Albuquerque: University of New Mexico Press, 1983), pp. 110-11. For the ongoing appeal of dude ranches, see Elizabeth Clair Flood, *Old-Time Dude Ranches Out West* (Salt Lake City: Gibbs Smith, 1995).

[39]   Wister, *The Virginian*, p. 399; Thomas H. Ince, "The Undergraduate and the Scenario," *Bookman* 47 (June 1918): 417; Arthur F. McClure and Ken Jones, *Western Films: Heroes, Heavies and Sagebrush of the "B" Genre* (South Brunswick: A. S. Barnes and Co., 1972), p. 14. See also the writer guidelines for *Bonanza*, in Rita Parks, *The Western Hero in Film and Television: Mass Media Mythology* (Ann Arbor: UMI Research Press, 1982), p. 163.

[40]   Wister, *The Virginian*, p. 13; Charles M. Russell, "Some Liars of the Old West," *Trails Plowed Under*, p. 191. The pair of prints, *The Poker Game* and *The End of the Poker Game at Hople's [Hop Lee's]*, are reproduced along with a related pair of Russell wax groups, in Rick Stewart, *Charles M. Russell, Sculptor* (Fort Worth: Amon Carter Museum, distributed by Harry N. Abrams, New York, 1994), pp. 18-19.

[41]   C. M. Rusell to Guy Weadick, April 7, 1925, *Word Painter*, pp. 374-75; and see Candace Savage, *Cowgirls* (Vancouver: Greystone Books, 1996); Maureen Christensen, "A Gun in Her Hands: Women in Firearms Advertising, 1900-1920," *Armax* 5 (1995): 7-88; and for bibliographical guidance, Dorothy Sloan—Books, Austin, TX, Cat. 3 (1986): *Women in the Cattle Country*.

[42]   Jon Tuska, *The Filming of the Great Westerns* (Garden City: Doubleday, 1976), pp. 438-44; Raymond William Stedman, *Shadows of the Indian: Stereotypes in American Culture* (Norman: University of Oklahoma Press, 1982), chap. 3; Ince, "The Undergraduate and the Scenario," p. 417.

[43]   See G. Edward White, *The Eastern Establishment and the Western Experience: The West of Frederic Remington, Theodore Roosevelt, and Owen Wister* (New Haven: Yale University Press, 1968); Brian W. Dippie, "Frederic Remington's Wild West," *American Heritage* 26 (April 1975): 13-15; and, for some insights, Alexander Nemerov, *Frederic Remington and Turn-of-the-Century America* (New Haven: Yale University Press, 1995).

[44]   Theodore Roosevelt, "Frontier Types," *Century Magazine* 36 (October 1888): 838; Wister, *The Virginian*, p. 48; Theodore Roosevelt, "Sheriff's Work on a Ranch," *Century Magazine* 36 (May 1888): 46.

[45]   Roosevelt, "Frontier Types," pp. 831-32, 843.

[46]   Walt Whitman, "One's-Self I Sing," *Leaves of Grass: The Collected Poems of Walt Whitman*, Emory Holloway, ed. (New York: Book League of America, 1942), p. 1; Elizabeth Johns, *American Genre Painting: The Politics of Everyday Life* (New Haven: Yale University Press, 1991), pp. 12, 203; Peter H. Hassrick, Introduction to *American Frontier Life: Early Western Painting and Prints* (New York: Abbeville Press, for the Amon Carter Museum, Fort Worth, and the Buffalo Bill Historical Center, Cody, WY, 1987), pp. 13-14.

[47]   Daryl Jones, *The Dime Novel Western* (Bowling Green, OH: Popular Press, 1978), p. 129

[48]   See Rick Stewart, Joseph D. Ketner II, and Angela L. Miller, *Carl Wimar: Chronicler of the Missouri River Frontier* (Fort Worth: Amon Carter Museum, distributed by Harry N. Abrams, New York, 1991).

[49]   Catlin, *Letters and Notes*, I: 18; and see Dippie, *Catlin and His Contemporaries, passim*.

[50]   See Carol Clark, "Charles Deas," in *American Frontier Life*, pp. 51-77.

[51]   Henry L. Dawes, March 26, 1884, *Congressional Record*, 48 Cong., 1 sess., and Theodore Roosevelt, First Annual Message, December 3, 1901, both quoted in Brian W. Dippie, *The Vanishing American: White Attitudes and U.S. Indian Policy* (Lawrence: University Press of Kansas, 1991 [1982]), pp. 196, 244.

[52]   Jim Kitses, *Horizons West: Anthony Mann, Budd Boetticher, Sam Peckinpah—Studies of Authorship within the Western* (Bloomington: Indiana University Press, 1970), p. 12; and for an extension of Kitses' analysis to television Westerns, see Ralph Brauer with Donna Brauer, *The Horse, The Gun and The Piece of Property: Changing Images of the TV Western* (Bowling Green, OH: Bowling Green University Popular Press, 1975). Their point is that the Western series ultimately denied open options and instead venerated stability and status.

[53]   Gene Autry, "Producing a Television Western," *Television Magazine*, October 1952, quoted in Brauer and Brauer, *The Horse, The Gun and The Piece of Property*, p. 26; and see John R. Hamilton (with John Calvin Batchelor), *Thunder in the Dust: Classic Images of Western Movies* (New York: Stewart, Tabori & Chang, 1987), pp. 102-121 for some Hollywood chases.

[54]   Frederic Remington to Eva Remington, November 6, 1900, *Frederic Remington—Selected Letters*, Allen P. Splete and Marilyn D. Splete, eds. (New York: Abbeville Press, 1988), p. 318; and see Linda Ayres, "William Ranney," and Warder H. Cadbury, "Arthur F. Tait," in *American Frontier Life*, pp. 79-129. For Faust and his views, see Robert Easton, *Max Brand: The Big "Westerner"* (Norman: University of Oklahoma Press, 1970), and Russel Nye, *The Unembarrassed Muse: The Popular Arts in America* (New York: Dial Press, 1970), p. 298.

[55]   Walt Whitman, "A Death-Sonnet for Custer," *New York Tribune*, July 10, 1876; and see Brian W. Dippie, *Custer's Last Stand: The Anatomy of an American Myth* (Lincoln: University of Nebraska Press, 1994 [1976]), and "'What Valor Is': Artists and the Mythic Moment," in *Legacy: New Perspectives on the Battle of the Little Bighorn*, Charles E. Rankin, ed. (Helena: Montana Historical Society Press, 1996), pp. 209-30; and Paul Andrew Hutton, "'Correct in Every Detail': General Custer in Hollywood," *ibid.*, pp. 231-70. Interestingly, Guy C. McElroy, *Facing History: The Black Image in American Art 1710-1940* (San Francisco: Bedford Arts, for the Corcoran Gallery of Art, Washington, DC, 1990), p. 100, finds that *Leaving the Canyon* exemplifies "Remington's vigorous portrayal of the African-American soldier."

[56]   C. M. Russell to Paris Gibson, February 4, 1902, *Good Medicine: The Illustrated Letters of Charles M. Russell* (Garden City: Doubleday, Doran, 1929), pp. 70-1; and, for Russell's composition, see Brian W. Dippie, "Charles M. Russell: The Artist in His Prime," in *Charles M. Russell: The Artist in His Heyday, 1903-1926* (Santa Fe: Gerald Peters Gallery, in association with Mongerson-Wunderlich, 1995), pp. 13-22.

[57]   [Mary F. Roberts], "Edward [sic] Willard Deming's Presentation of Indian Subjects at the Snedecor Gallery," *Craftsman* 21 (January 1912): 456; Richard H. Pratt, quoted in M. E. Gates, "Land and Law as Agents in Educating Indians," *Journal of Social Science* 21 (September 1886): 131; and see "Folk-lore of a Vanishing Race Preserved in the Paintings of Edwin Willard Deming—Artist-Historian of the American Indian," *Craftsman* 10 (May 1906): 150-67; "Mural Painting in This Country since 1898," *Scribner's Magazine* 40 (November 1906): 637-40; and Dippie, *Vanishing American*, chap. 13. As neighbors, Deming and James E. Fraser were both featured in P. T. Farnsworth, "The Artists' Colony in Macdougal Alley, Where Some of Our Best Known American Painters and Sculptors Live and Work," *Craftsman* 11 (October 1906): 57-69.

[58]   Stephen Crane, *The Red Badge of Courage and Other Writings*, Richard Chase, ed. (Boston: Houghton Mifflin [Riverside Editions], 1960), p. 388; Perriton Maxwell, "Frederic Remington—Most Typical of American Artists," *Pearson's Magazine* 18 (October 1907): 407. *Fight for the Waterhole* is also known under the title *An Arizona Water Hole*; for a variant interpretation of its meaning, see Alex Nemerov, "Doing the 'Old America'": The Image of the American West, 1880-1920," in *The West as America: Reinterpreting Images of the Frontier, 1820-1920*, William H. Truettner, ed. (Washington, DC: Smithsonian Institution Press, for the National Museum of American Art, 1991),

pp. 284-343, and his *Frederic Remington and Turn-of-the-Century America*, pp. 10-16, 74-5. The first extended interpretive study to deal with Remington's darkening vision is Ben Merchant Vorpahl, *Frederic Remington and the West: With the Eye of the Mind* (Austin: University of Texas Press, 1978).

59   See Susan Danly and Leo Marx, *The Railroad in American Art: Representations of Technological Change* (Cambridge: MIT Press, 1988); and Brian W. Dippie, "The Moving Finger Writes: Western Art and the Dynamics of Change," in Jules David Prown, et al., *Discovered Lands, Invented Pasts: Transforming Visions of the American West* (New Haven: Yale University Press, 1992), pp. 96-99.

60   Walt Whitman, "Pioneers! O Pioneers!" (1865, 1881) and "Passage to India" (1868, 1871), *Leaves of Grass*, pp. 195, 344-45. Also interesting on the proposition that "these States tend inland and toward the western sea" and the idea of "the circle almost circled" are "A Promise to California" (1860, 1867), pp. 108-09, and "Facing West from California's Shores" (1860, 1867), p. 94.

61   Patricia Nelson Limerick, *The Legacy Of Conquest: The Unbroken Past of the American West* (New York: W. W. Norton, 1987); Richard White, "Trashing the Trails," in *Trails: Toward a New Western History*, Patricia Nelson Limerick, Clyde A. Milner II, and Charles E. Rankin, eds. (Lawrence: University Press of Kansas, 1991), pp. 26-39.

62   See John P. Hart, "Contemporary Perspectives on the Little Bighorn," and Edward T. Linenthal, "From Shrine to Historic Site: The Little Bighorn Battlefield National Monument," in *Legacy*, pp. 271-85, 307-19; C. Richard King, "Segregated Stories: The Colonial Contours of the Little Bighorn Battlefield National Monument," in *Dressing in Feathers: The Construction of the Indian in American Popular Culture*, S. Elizabeth Bird, ed. (Boulder, CO Westview Press, 1996), pp. 167-80; and James Brooke, "Culture Clash: Battle at Devils Tower," *Times Colonist* (Victoria, BC), July 13, 1997 (from the *New York Times*).

63   Walter Truett Anderson, Introduction to Greg MacGregor, *Overland: The California Emigrant Trail of 1841-1870* (Albuquerque: University of New Mexico Press, 1996), p. xvi. Also worthy of note are *Revealing Territory: Photographs of the Southwest by Mark Klett* (Albuquerque; University of New Mexico Press, 1992) and Drex Brooks, *Sweet Medicine: Sites of Indian Massacres, Battlefields, and Treaties* (Albuquerque: University of New Mexico Press, 1995), for their photographs of a Western land that cannot be divorced from its human presence and the meanings that presence lends it, and for their accompanying interpretive essays. The work of MacGregor, Klett, et al. necessarily partakes of irony, but the guiding spirit is sympathetic. Others approach the task with an arch, unflattering eye: for example, Richard Avedon, *In the American West: 1979-1984* (New York: Harry N. Abrams, 1985), which reduces the Western dream to so much human flotsam and jetsam, rootless, defeated, drifting across a blank space. In contrast, *Passing Through: Western Meditations of Douglas Kent Hall* (Flagstaff, AZ: Northland Publishing, 1989) offers variety and range in its portrayal of Western types, from the famous to the obscure, and from winners to losers. Richard Ansaldi's *Souvenirs from the Roadside West* (New York: Harmony Books, 1978) constitutes an affectionate "personal collection" of Southwestern tourist images, while Fritz Scholder's *Indian Kitsch: The Use and Misuse of Indian Images* (Flagstaff, AZ: Northland Press, in cooperation with the Heard Museum, 1979), has more bite, as its title indicates, and throws a revealing light on Scholder's artistic concerns. His art combines parody and homage—evident in a painting like *Matinee Cowboy, Posing* (1978), a tribute to his boyhood hero Monte Hale that erases the lines in the game of cowboys and Indians. Mark Klett earlier (1977-82) contributed to a Rephotographic Survey Project that matched nineteenth century views with photographs made today from the same locations. Others have done similar comparative surveys with different ends in mind. Donald R. Progulske and Richard H. Sowell's *Yellow Ore, Yellow Hair, Yellow Pine: A Photographic Study of a Century of Forest Ecology* (Brookings: South Dakota State University, Agricultural Experiment Station, Bulletin 616, July 1974) matched present-day views with those made by William H. Illingworth on George A. Custer's Black Hills Expedition in 1874 "to show man's impact on the Black Hills, a natural forest in western South Dakota and eastern Wyoming." Inspired, historian Paul L. Hedren retraced photographer Stanley L. Morrow's steps in *With Crook in the Black Hills: Stanley J. Morrow's 1876 Photographic Legacy* (Boulder, CO: Pruett Publishing, 1985). One impressive rephotographic project undertaken by Klett in 1990 involved matching a

panorama of San Francisco made by Eadweard Muybridge in 1878—and, the challenge, as Klett notes, speaks to the old problem of Western perspective. The horizontality of plains and desert that challenged the artist in the nineteenth century complemented Muybridge's task, since his version of the magisterial gaze—the view from the height with the city spread out below—was relatively easily attained in 1878, but is denied the modern photographer by the highrises that now dominate the cityscape. In the twentieth century, verticality has replaced horizontality as one Western artist's problem, reflecting a fact of Western development that today, in percentage terms, more Westerners live in cities than any other group of Americans. See Eadweard Muybridge and Mark Klett, *One City/Two Visions: San Francisco Panoramas, 1878 and 1990* (San Francisco: Bedgord Arts, 1990).

[64]   Elliott West, "A Longer, Grimmer, but More Interesting Story," in *Trails*, pp. 103-11; and see Richard White and Patricia Nelson Limerick, *The Frontier in American Culture*, James R. Grossman, ed. (Berkeley: University of California Press, 1994), for White on Buffalo Bill and the turn-of-the-century Western myth, and for Limerick on coming to terms with the "f" word, "frontier."

[65]   Catlin, *Letters and Notes*, I: 261-62; "The Proposed National Park in the Yellowstone Country," *Frank Leslie's Illustrated Newspaper* 33 (March 2 1872): 398.

[66]   George Catlin to The Editor of the Herald: "The Great Park of the Yellow Stone," draft letter, George Catlin Papers, Archives of American Art, Smithsonian Institution, Washington, DC, Roll No. 2136; Roderick Nash, *Wilderness and the American Mind* (New Haven: Yale University Press, 1967), pp. vii, 236; and see H. Duane Hampton, *How the U.S. Cavalry Saved Our National Parks* (Bloomington: Indiana University Press, 1971), and Lee H. Whittlesey's eye-opening *Death in Yellowstone: Accidents and Foolhardiness in the First National Park* (Niwot, Co: Roberts Rinehart, 1995).

[67]   See Earl Pomeroy, *In Search of the Golden West: The Tourist in Western America* (New York: Alfred A. Knopf, 1957), chap. 3; *After the Buffalo Were Gone: Louis W. Hill, Sr., and the Blackfeet at Glacier National Park* (St. Paul: Science Museum of Minnesota, [1985]); Alfred Runte, *Trains of Discovery: Western Railroads and the National Parks* (Niwot, CO: Roberts Rinehart, 1994); and Mark Spence, "Dispossessing the Wilderness: Yosemite Indians and the National Park Ideal, 1864-1930," *Pacific Historical Review* 65 (February 1996): 27-59.

[68]   Anne Farrar Hyde, *An American Vision: Far Western Landscape and National Culture, 1820-1920* (New York: New York University Press, 1990), chap. 6; Jack Ellis Haynes, *Yellowstone Stage Holdups* (Bozeman, MT: Haynes Studios, 1959), pp. 5, 15-20, 27; Harry B. Mitchell to James B. Rankin, November 2, 1937, James B. Rankin Papers, Montana Historical Society, Helena; and see Susan C. Scofield and Jeremy C. Schmidt, *The Inn at Old Faithful* (n.p.: Crowsnest Associates, 1979).

[69]   Roy W. Meyer, "B. M. Bower: The Poor Man's Wister," *Journal of Popular Culture* 7 (Winter 1973): 672.

[70]   Brauer and Brauer, *The Horse, The Gun and The Piece of Property*, pp. 9-10; Kevin Brownlow, *The War, the West, and the Wilderness* (New York: Alfred A. Knopf, 1979), pp. 220-399; *Life Savers Book-O-Stars* (Port Chester, NY: Life Savers Inc., 1931); and see Paul E. Mix, *The Life and Legend of Tom Mix* (South Brunswick: A. S. Barnes and Company, 1972), p. 104; and Olive Stokes Mix, with Eric Heath, *The Fabulous Tom Mix* (Englewood Cliffs, NJ: Prentice-Hall, 1957), p. 138: "His extravagance became almost a disease." He filled his Beverly Hills mansion with the trophies of his cowboy fame—"countless ornamental saddles and silver-encrusted bridles; an arsenal of rifles and revolvers; his enormous collection of spurs, sombreros, ribbons, medals and loving cups. These trophies, all manifestations and symbols of his past life—the life that he was constantly reaching back to look for—were egregiously out of place among the expensive pieces of imported furniture . . ." Jones is well-covered in Tuska, *The Filming of the West*, and Brownlow, *The War, the West, and the Wilderness*. The question remains: Can you indeed have airplanes and Westerns all in one? The essence of the Western, the Brauers argue, is anti-technology. Technology is no match for men and horses—or for the elements. Of course there is something absurdly Luddite in all this. Aficionados of

the railroad train viewed the advent of the age of the airplane with the same nervous apprehension Indians exhibited towards railroad trains in nineteenth-century allegorical art. The cover illustration for one popular railroad magazine in 1941 showed a snowy evening, a downed aircraft, and passengers calmly filing off, briefcases and purses in hand, to climb up an embankment towards a waiting train whose piercing light, cutting through the darkness and the falling snow, was still the light of the future for those who dreamed of an unchanging past (*Grounded*, by Albin Henning, *Railroad Magazine* 29 [February 1941]). The Western was always threatened with irrelevance. After Charles Lindbergh's solo flight across the Atlantic, the lone hero seemed to have found a new home in the skies and contemporaries were pronouncing the death of the Western. But the death of the Western has itself become a timeless theme. See Parks, *The Western Hero in Film and Television*, p. 155; and John W. Ward, "The Meaning of Lindbergh's Flight," *American Quarterly* 10 (Spring 1958): 3-16.

[71]   William W. Savage, Jr., *Comic Books and America, 1945-1954* (Norman: University of Oklahoma Press, 1990), p. 69.

[72]   Wister, *The Virginian*, p. 253.

[73]   Harry Carr, *Los Angeles: City of Dreams* (New York: Grosset & Dunlap, 1935), p. 345; Joe De Yong to Mary De Yong, March 17, March 20, March 3, 1924, De Yong Papers; Robert L. Cotton, "Joe De Yong: 'Artist from A to Z,'" *Old West* 9 (Winter 1972): 34; and see Kevin Starr, *Inventing the California Dream: California through the Progressive Era* (New York: Oxford University Press, 1985), pp. 82-5 .

[74]   W. W. Robinson, "The Real Estate Boom of the Twenties," in *Los Angeles: Biography of a City*, John and Laree Caughey, eds. (Berkeley: University of California Press, 1976), p. 277; Edgar Lloyd Hampton, "Los Angeles, a Miracle City," *Current History* 24 (April 1926): 35, 42.

[75]   C. M. Russell to Berners B. Kelly, Feb 22, 1920, and to James R. Hobbins, February 26, 1920, *Word Painter*, pp. 288, 290.

[76]   C. M. Russell to Douglas Fairbanks, April 27, 1921, private collection; and C. M. Russell to Charles F. Lummis, May 7, 1922, *Word Painter*, p. 322.

[77]   Wallace D. Coburn, "Passing Trails" (April 10, 1917, typescript, Britzman; Walter J. Coburn to Frank Bird Linderman, Frank Bird Linderman Collection, Maureen and Mike Mansfield Library, University of Montana, Missoula; E. C. "Teddy Blue" Abbott to Charles M. Russell, February 1, 1926, Britzman; C. M. Russell to Editor of *Adventure*, March 7, 1924, *Word Painter*, p. 343.

[78]   Western literature has enjoyed close and sympathetic attention, but what Wallace Stegner called the large "W" Western—the formula fiction—is another matter. In contrast to the relatively lofty place Western movies have held in film studies (thanks in part, no doubt, to the enthusiasm of French cineastes), the Western formula fiction produced for a mass audience has not received much respect. Christine Bold's *Selling the Wild West: Popular Western Fiction, 1860-1960* (Bloomington: Indiana University Press, 1987) takes the formula fiction seriously, and makes a case for those writers who successfully asserted their individuality by subverting the formulas within which they worked. Her argument anticipates recent deconstructionist, and especially feminist, readings designed to uncover the Western's underlying cultural meanings, for example, Jane Tompkins, *West of Everything: The Inner Life of Westerns* (New York: Oxford University Press, 1992), and Norris Yates, *Gender and Genre: An Introduction to Women Writers of Formula Westerns, 1900-1950* (Albuquerque: University of New Mexico Press, 1995). Back in 1864 William Everett, writing in the *North American Review* [99 (October 1864)]: 308, observed of the proliferation of dime novels, "Why these works are popular is a problem quite as much for the moralist and the student of national character as for the critic"—a prophetic statement considering the scholarly effort that has been expended searching out the Western's cultural implications. Students of popular culture have had a longstanding interest in the formula Western. See, for example, Nye, *The Unembarrassed Muse*, chap. 12, and John G. Cawelti, *The Six-Gun Mystique*

(Bowling Green, OH: Bowling Green University Popular Press, [1971]). The sheer quantity of formula Western fiction renders any discussion necessarily superficial, but useful surveys include Jones, *The Dime Novel Western*, and John A. Dinan, *The Pulp Western: A Popular History of the Western Fiction Magazine in America* (San Bernardino: Borgo Press, 1983). Dinan indicates the magnitude of the challenge awaiting a would-be student of Western pulp fiction by listing the titles of magazines published from the 1920s through the 1940s devoted exclusively to Western stories —182 in all, some published weekly! Two practitioners of the art have told their stories: Frank Gruber, *The Pulp Jungle* (Los Angeles: Sherbourne Press, 1967) and Walt Coburn, *Western Word Wrangler: An Autobiography* (Flagstaff, AZ: Northland Press, 1973). Based on his experience, Gruber concluded that there were only seven basic Western plots, a thesis he advanced in "The Basic Western Novel Plots," *Writer's 1955 Year Book* (No. 26): 49-53, 160, and defended in his autobiography, since every eighth plot sent him in the intervening years fit into one of his original seven. Some context is provided by Ron Goulart, *Cheap Thrills: An Informal History of the Pulp Magazines* (New Rochelle, NY: Arlington House, 1972). The Western appeared in every form of media; see Jim Harmon, *The Great Radio Heroes* (Garden City: Doubleday, 1967), which includes Tom Mix and the Lone Ranger, and Maurice Horn, *Comics of the American West* (New York: Winchester Press, 1977). Useful for negotiating the flow from fiction into film (nothing comparable yet exists for the flow from art into filmic imagery, though students have explored the relationship between Remington's art and John Ford's Western imagery) is Jim Hitt, *The American West from Fiction (1823-1976) into Film (1909-1986)* (Jefferson, NC: McFarland, 1990). Hitt cites Walt Coburn as an example of a relationship he acknowledges but does not choose to explore, that between mass-producers of pulp Western stories and the movies adapted from their work, since the pulp writers have had "little overall effect on the genre except to give it a bad name" (p. viii)—a strange judgment in the land of Zane Grey and Max Brand. Hitt's selectivity is mitigated by a useful appendix listing "Western Authors and Their Film Adaptations." Books on Western film constitute a library unto themselves. Two massive studies full of firsthand information are Tuska, *The Filming of the West*, and Brownlow, *The War, the West, and the Wilderness*. Following the fan magazines, many books on the Western are devoted to the stars and their sidekicks; others are concerned with Western directors. John Wayne and John Ford occupy a bookcase between them. Some are reference books, listing titles and credits and providing plot synopses; several are theoretical exegeses of the genre. Cultural studies use film to examine the portrayal of the cowboy and the Indian on screen, as well as legendary individuals and events. Jesse James, Billy the Kid, Wyatt Earp, Custer's Last Stand and the Alamo have all been done. A few of the books on the Western are broad-based cultural histories intended to link film to general trends in American culture. In that respect, George N. Fenin and William K. Everson, *The Western: From Silents to the Seventies* (New York: Grossman, 1973), an expanded edition of the 1962 original, is still not superseded, though it tends to be singleminded in judging Westerns by the standard of authenticity. As Rita Parks wrote in *The Western Hero in Film and Television*, p. 1: "It is one of the basic assumptions of this study that what is true—that is, internally consistent—often goes beyond what is factual to create a reality more genuine than the fact can hope to produce . . . . The historical fact is the existence of the Man of the West; the legend is the myth of the Western hero." As for the linkage between Western art and film in terms of Western imagery, a promising pathway consists of Western parodies. *The Little Train Robbery* followed *The Great Train Robbery* (1903), from the same studio, by just two years. Two early Westerns, the first a parody—*Wild and Wooly* (1917), written by Anita Loos and starring Douglas Fairbanks, and *Hell Bent* (1918), directed by John Ford and starring Harry Carey—used Remington paintings coming to life as storytelling devices. No better direct evidence for the influence of Western art on Western film will be found. See James H. Nottage, "Authenticity and Western Film," *Gilcrease Journal* 1 (Spring 1993): 54-66.

[79]   C. M. Russell to Frank Brown, April 4, 1926, *Word Painter*, p. 388; C. M. Russell to Bart Noble, April 11, 1926, typescript, Rankin Papers.

[80]   C. M. Russell to Edward Borein, February 13, 1918, *Word Painter*, p. 247; Harold G. Davidson, *Jimmy Swinnerton: The Artist and His Work* (New York: Hearst Books, 1985), pp. 85, 93; Katherine Lipke, "Art of Russell Is Red Blooded," Los Angeles *Times*, March 30, 1924. In a letter to another artist, Joe Scheuerle [February 1918], *Word Painter*, p. 248, Russell qualified his Southwestern enthusiasm: "it is a great country wild and makes good picture stuff. the Indians are not as good as there northern brothers eather in looks ore dress but a bunch of Navajoes mounted in there country of red sand makes a good picture and for a man who likes mountians and

Indians I know no better country." Without getting into the Taos School as such, three books are useful in understanding the relationship between tourism and the artistic discovery of the Southwest: T. C. McLuhan, *Dream Tracks: The Railroad and the American Indian 1890-1930* (New York: Harry N. Abrams, 1985); Sandra D'Emilio and Suzan Campbell, *Visions & Visionaries: The Art & Artists of the Santa Fe Railway* (Salt Lake City: Gibbs Smith, 1991); and Kathleen L. Howard and Diana F. Pardu, *Inventing the Southwest: The Fred Harvey Company and Native American Art* (Flagstaff, AZ: Northland Publishing, for the Heard Museum, Phoenix, 1996).

[81]   C. M. Russell to Will James, May 12, 1920, in William Gardner Bell, *Will James: The Life and Works of a Lone Cowboy* (Flagstaff, AZ: Northland Press, 1987), p. 47; C. M. Russell to Charles A. Beil, May 31, 1926, *Word Painter*, p. 393.

[82]   Harrison Rhodes, "Is There a West?," *Harper's Monthly* 141 (June 1920): 70, 72.

[83]   Mark Thistlewaite, "The Most Important Themes: History Painting and Its Place in American Art," in William H. Gerdts and Mark Thistlewaite, *Grand Illusions: History Painting in America* (Fort Worth: Amon Carter Museum, 1988), p. 44; Nathanael West, *Miss Lonelyhearts & The Day of the Locust* (New York: New Directions Paperbook, 1962), pp. 157, 165, 60.

[84]   Diana Serra Cary, *The Hollywood Posse: The Story of a Gallant Band of Horsemen Who Made Movie History* (Boston: Houghton Mifflin, 1975), p. 145; "The World's Greatest City—In Prospect," *World's Work* 47 (December 1923): 140-41. It seems likely that Cary misremembered in naming Pawnee Bill; no corroboration is provided by Glenn Shirley, *Pawnee Bill: A Biography of Major Gordon W. Lillie* (Albuquerque: University of New Mexico Press, 1958). But there were enough veterans of the Indian wars living in California—and storied scouts like Luther S. "Yellowstone" Kelly—to form a battalion. James Willard Schultz, author of the classic memoir *My Life as an Indian* (1907) spent many summers in Blackfoot country, but his winters ordinarily found him in Southern California. The examples could be multiplied.

[85]   E. C. "Teddy Blue" Abbott to C. M. Russell, February 1, 1926, Britzman; C. M. Russell to Edward Borein [mid-March 1926], *Word Painter*, p. 384.